Independent Television News Limited   **ITN House 48**

Phone: 01-637 2424
Telex: 22101
Cables: Telindep London PS4

The Reader
Monty Python's Big Red Book

Monday

Dear Monty Python Reader

I am extremely pleased that you have decided to buy this book as I personally
think it's the best book in the world with one or two exceptions. I can
thoroughly and almost wholeheartedly recommend it to nearly anyone who quite
likes this sort of thing. I haven't read anything that is much funnier for
several weeks.

As you know, I'm not the sort of chap who goes around recommending anything or
anyone, and the reason I'm doing this is quite simple. Another thing, all the
lads at ITN enjoy a good laugh and they too join me in wishing you all the best
of luck in getting laughs out of this material.

All the best,

Reginald Bosanquet

Reginald Bosanquet

*Is this alright?
(Incidentally, I thought
the book a bit long — can
you cut it a little, or a lot?
Looking forward to your cheque)
Do you think Methuen would
be interested in a News at Ten
Book?
Regards
RB*

Directors: Julian Aymes James Bredin Aubrey Buxton MC Norman Collins Sir Geoffrey Cox CBE Donald I Edwards CBE Dr Tom Margerison
Howard Thomas CBE C D Wilson CBE MC

Independent Television News Limited ITN House 48 Wells Street London W1P 3FE

Phone 01–637–2424
Telex: 2/2101
Cables: Telindep London PS4

Wednesday

Python Productions Ltd,
8 Waterloo Place,
Pall Mall,
S.W.1.

Dear Sirs,

    Leonard Parkin, Jackie Gillot, Gordon Honeycombe,
Ivor Mills, Peter Sissons, Gerald Seymour, Peter Fairley,
Sandy Gall and all here at ITN wish to make it clear that we
are in no way associated with R. Bosanquet's endorsement of
your rather silly book.

               Yours sincerely,

               Andrew Gardner.

    P.S. Do you think Methuen <u>would</u> be interested in a News
At Ten Book?

Directors: Julian Aymes Aubrey Buxton W H Cheevers Norman Collins Sir Geoffrey Cox Donald I Edwards Dr. Tom Margerison Howard Thomas C D Wilson

"Dunordrin",
13, Buzz Aldrin Cres.,
Hitler,
Surrey.

From:
Colonel "Sandy" Volestrangler.

Dear Readers,

I would like to point out the trouble which the Python team have got themselves into by not asking me to write their Foreword. They've obviously got themselves into no end of bother, and perhaps even expensive litigation, with these profess- ional newscasters, instead of sticking to endorsements from fictitious characters like myself. Now I'm not offended, well, perhaps just a little, as I have helped them on one or two of their programmes when things were getting a little dull, and my wife and Captain Johnson both said I was terribly good, so you can probably understand how I might be a little disappointed with the noticeable lack of any formal request to write anything for them.

Had I been asked to write their Foreword - and I haven!t,so there it is,enough said,let's just allow it to pass unmentioned - had they been courteous enough to ask me to write a small Foreword (and it needn't have been a long one,I would have been quite prepared to keep it short and make any cuts they liked) had they done me this small courtesy as a kind of 'thank-you' for all the hard work I've put into the series,I should undoubtedly probably have said yes. However they haven't,so the answer must remain a mystery.

If I ever had to write a Foreword for anybody or anything,say a book, or something like that,and incidentally I never have,I should probably say that the Army is one of the finest fighting forces in Britain today. I should add,in this hypothetical Foreword (just for argumen's sake let's say it was a Foreword for what? say a Monty Python book) I should that the army was one of the finest possible influences on a young chaps life. It certainly made a man of me. And it made a man of my wife. However I haven't been asked to write any Foreword so let it pass.

I would like to wish this book the success it deserves,forgetting any slight,real or imagined,that certain persons may feel. Also I should like to say that I bear no personal grudge whatever towards Reginald Bosanquet just because he got the plum job of writing the Foreword and not me or anybody else perhaps more appropriate.

Sincerely,

(Colonel "Sandy" Volestrangler) (Mrs)

P.S. If anybody does need a Foreword perhaps they would contact me?

BRITISH BROADCASTING CORPORATION

TELEVISION CENTRE   WOOD LANE   LONDON W12

TELEPHONE 01-743 8000   CABLES: BROADCASTS LONDON PS4

TELEGRAMS: BROADCASTS LONDON TELEX   TELEX: 22182

Dear Python,

I am writing to say how disappointed we all are here at the BBC, in that having worked for the Corporation you should have sought endorsement for your book from Independent Television Newscasters rather than the BBC's own Newsreaders.

Robert Dougall, Kenneth Kendall and I would all have been perfectly willing to write a much better Foreword than Reginald Bosanquet, whoever he is, subject to the usual terms and conditions, and probably for less.

No wonder the BBC are suspicious of you.

Yours faithfully,

Richard Baker

(Richard Baker)

P.S. Do you think Methuen would be interested in a Nine o'Clock News Book?

P.P.S. If we included Michael Aspel would they?

POST ~~~~ OFFICE

8 SW1 +   TSO TGMS LN

TELEGRAM

Prefix. Time handed in. Office of Origin and Service Instructions. Words.

At_____ m

From_____

By_____

=✝H248 5.15 LONDON T 28

OVERNIGHT PYTHON PRODUCTIONS 8 WATERLOO PLACE SW1 =

APPALLED BY YOUR LACK OF TASTE IN NOT CHOOSING A
STAFF NEWSCASTER TO WRITE THE FOREWORD = RONALD
FLETCHER BBC SOUND RADIO +

POST ~~~~

8 SW1 2 +   TSO TGMS L

TELEGRAM

Prefix. Time handed in. Office of Origin and Service Instructions. Words.

At_____

From_____ m

By_____

✝H249 5.13 LONDON T 28

OVERNIGHT PYTHON PRODUCTIONS 8 WATERLOO PLACE SW1 =

JUST BECAUSE WE ARE A MINORITY CHANNEL IT DOESNT
MEAN WE CANT WRITE FOREWORDS STOP DEEPLY OFFENDED =
PETER WOODS BBC2 NEWSROOM +

BRITISH BROADCASTING CORPORATION
TELEVISION CENTRE WOOD LANE LONDON W12
TELEPHONE 01-743 8000   CABLES: BROADCASTS LONDON PS4
TELEGRAMS: BROADCASTS LONDON TELEX   TELEX: 22182

Date as postmark.

From the Managing Director.

Dear John, Eric, Michael, Graham and Terry,

I have been asked by the Head of Regional News to pass on several
complaints he has received from the Regions about Python using
an ITN Newscaster as a Foreword writer.

I must say I agree with him.

Yours,

Huw Wheldon.
(Managing Director, Television)

P.S. I myself am available for any future Forewords, Cabaret
or Masonics.

P.P.S. Do you think Methuen would be interested in a book about
Managing Directors of Television ?

OLIDAYS are fun in our new range
citing swimwear. Yes! you too can
e sensation of the beach this Summer
uly 39/6. Also please come home
orie, the kids miss you – love Ted
aging Director, **SWIMMEX**
MWEAR LTD.)

OETS! Poets are needed by a
table publisher to fill a new annual of
s for this year. Why not send **your**
s for a critical appreciation and the
ce of **World-Wide publication to:**
ary Poetical Undertakings Ltd., Rip
overnment Surplus Town,
ex.

AVE ££££££££££££! Why pay over
MES as much as you need? Don't
OW YOUR MONEY AWAY! Why be
OL? You may be **CRAZY** but you
need to look such a **STUPID GIT!** I
you **STINK!** Yah boo! Why don't
go and **JUMP IN A VAT OF YOUR**
EXCREMENT? The Bargain Centre,
es.

ICESTER WRITER'S

Outrageous TV Scripts

Read his frank views on comedy on the box in this week's

am Chapman,
ter extraordinary

eicester Chronicle

● ON SALE ALL NEWSAGENTS – FRIDAY ●

OOK up an old friend this evening!
son's New **IMPROVED "Straddle"**
ator can raise practically anybody 4
off the ground. Write for **FREE**
ure and a lunch with the director:
son & Jones Ltd. Waverly Building,
vich.

HY NOT be different this Christmas?
not send your friends a lump of cold
It may cost less than you think!
e to: **"VOM-IT"** Products, 13,
rth Road, Preston, Lancs. Sole
s: Mr. & Mrs. Ernie Scrotem.

BAD SPELLING

ing ruins your chances more. ualified teacher can help you. details sent in confidence.

LOOSE COVER FOR YOU! Yes! At
we can offer a complete range of
e-knitted loose covers, made to fit
self or any relative. These are a
T for people who tend to remain
onary for long periods. **STOPS dust**
ng into the cracks and crevices that
re left unprotected. Fit a loose cover
yourself today! Lamprey Loose
rs, Ltd. The Dales, Wonersh.

OURMETS!! Your chance to try
L Turkish "Samarvi" the fabled
acy of Kublai Khan. (Don't be put
its appearance). Write now for a
sample to: **"VOM-IT"** Products, 13,
rth Road, Preston, Lancs. Sole
s: Mr. & Mrs Ernie Scrotem.

ANOS repaired and put in little
board boxes. **WE ARE EXPERTS.**
nily business since 1869. Avoid all
tions. The Pianos Into Little
board Boxes Ltd. 268, Dagworth
Bolton.

● **CLEANS LIKE MAGIC!** Try the amazing **NEW carpet-cleaner "ATOM-CLEEN"**. It's **FANTASTIC!** Cleans in **A FLASH!** (Don't be put off by its smell) write now for a free sample to: **"VOM-IT"** PRODUCTS, 13 Elgarth Road, Preston, Lancs. Sole Props.: Mr. & Mrs. Ernie Scrotem.

MUSCLES

Made Easy

Send for **FREE** Booklet

I was a 7-stone weakling until I discovered "**DYNAMIC-TENSION**" the secret method of developing REAL MEN. Send for my free book and details of my 7-day FREE trial offer.

FREE! booklet

Name ....
Address ....
....
Age ....

CUT ALONG DOTTED LINE

● **THE DELILAH** Body-Building Course . . . Put on muscles in interesting places. James Cagney of Altringham writes: "I never knew I had a muscle there until I took your **DELILAH** body-building course, and now I have two. I can also pick up a mug of cocoa with my left ear." **Write TODAY: Delilah body-building, Brighton.**

● **HOLIDAY HOMES** for dogs, cats, little furry hamsters – anything that moves. Send your pet in a cardboard box to: **THE HOLIDAY HOMES FOR PETS PIE CO. LTD.** Portsmouth.

● **FOR SALE:** upper lip, forearm, and knee-cap of ex-Life-Guard. Will do odd jobs around the house. **Write: P.O. Box 301**

● **MEN IT CAN BE DONE!** Horace Stokes did it last night! Write for photographic evidence: Mrs H. Stokes, 14, Belmont Crescent, Portugal.

LEATHER FLYING HELMET

For those who want the genuine article! As worn by wartime pilots. *Real Leather Sizes: Large, Medium or Small.* **Colour Dark Brown.**

£1.50 POST FREE

● **There's** nothing quite like a genuine Regency commode – at least there wasn't until we brought out our **FANTASTIC** reproduction one. So why not send now for one of our **wonderful walnut Regency Commodes**, based on a design created especially for Louis XIVth inlaid with genuine hand-carved marquetry and tooled with gold leaf, this piece of furniture will be a beautiful adornment to your home. (You can soon clean out the stuff inside it). Send to: **"VOM-IT" PRODUCTS**, 13 Elgarth Road, Preston, Lancs. Sole Props.: Mr. & Mrs. Ernie Scrotem.

● **FOR SALE:** tin of boot polish, part-used. Willing to exchange for 1964 Rolls Royce in Maroon or Royal Blue. Must have M.O.T. Write: Ron Hopeful, The Cut, Bishop's Stortford.

● **FOR SALE:** Desirable property in Neasden. Immaculate condit. Blonde hair. Will do anything. Write: c/o The Halifax Building Soc. Upper Bute St.

● **WANTED:** quiet time with a table lamp. No reasonable offer refused. P.O. Box 54302

● **LOST!** 3 storied, semi. det. res. 3 beds. 2 recep. 2 bath. Last seen: Sunday night. Please phone: Jill & Donald, 273 89975

● **LOOKING FOR A SAFE JOB?** We're doing one on Friday. Contact Stan, Nobby, Brian, and little Butch.

● **WHY** throw away those unwanted undergarments? Why not send them direct to: Reg. Cattermole, 136 The Buildings, Prestatyn.

● **FOR SALE:** Large bed-ridden female, keen on astrology and the re-establishment of diplomatic relations with Communist China.

● **Will part-exchange for slim brunette** with slightest interest in development of trade with emergent African nations. PO BOX ZZZZZZZ

● **FOR SALE:** Parrot. Likes children, but will make do with cuttlefish and a bit of grass seed. Write: BOX 15263645373-84756475857564748590298576253416-352718273645381

● **HOLIDAY** in Spain? Why not come to Cleethorpes? We've got everything the bloody Dagos have got, plus you don't have to learn their stupid language. "Cleethorpes – a good place for liberal intellectuals".

● **WANTED:** 3rd bach. share flt. Own cooking, use of bath and cat. Must be over 5ft, blonde, good-looking. Oh what a giveaway.

● **WINDOWS BROKEN!** Deposit accounts smeared with lard! Ring: Ted & Arthur Irresponsible, 278 5481.

● **NOW!** The **OFFER** you have been **WAITING FOR:** Fighter bombers for only £40. Will carry nuclear payload. Ring: Mrs. Lewis 048 39719 after 6pm.

LOOK ! UNBEATABLE VALUE ! ! !

BARGAIN ASSORTMENTS

FOR THE HANDYMAN OR TRADESMAN

IDEAL D.I.Y. GIFT

PACK No. 1, 1000 WOOD SCREWS. CSK. HD steel. Popular sizes ⅜"-2" separately packed. New. Finest quality.
PACK No. 2, BRASS WOOD SCREWS. CSK. HD. Over 300 in popular sizes ⅜"-1½" separately packed.
PACK No. 3, NAILS, PANEL PINS, TACKS, etc. A most useful assortment containing Rd & Oval wire nails ¾"-3", panel pins ⅝"-1½", hardboard nails and tacks. All items separately packed.

C.W.O. **£1.25** each

● **1958** Morris for sale. Really **VERY GOOD.** Although it doesn't sound it, I must say. But really it's **QUITE ALRIGHT.** Oh I know the back door doesn't shut properly, but once you've got the knack it's fairly easy. It's only £80 after all. Oh alright £70. Ring: Sid Letchworth 0000001 Oh alright £60.

● **Small** brown and green thing for sale. Could be a Vermeer. £5 O.N.D. BOX 213.

● **TOP PRICES PAID** for anything. RING: J. R. Silly 068 7564 54.

● **BUZZ ALDRIN MODELS.** Have a life-sized model of America's No. 2 Spaceman in your living-room! Says: "Hi! I'm Buzz", and produces sample of Moon rock. Ring: **NASA, HOUSTON, TEXAS.** Houston 2435645345 After 7.30pm

AS SHAPELY AS EVE

This is the bra which gives you that exciting cleavage, combined with a low plunge neckline.
Booster pads in the side of the cup gently press the bosom upwards and together. The front fastening is adjustable to your mood and desires. Made from nylon and lace, sizes 32" to 42", black or white. **Matching lace sideless panty 45p.** Free catalogue with order.

ONLY £1.35 P&P 9p
includes booster pads

● **GOING AWAY THIS YEAR?** Be sure to let **US** know – Ken & Alfie Stoat Box 813 Block A.

● **DON'T THROW AWAY** your old jam-jars. Send them to Mrs Betty Dago, 18a Leytonstone High St., and she will throw them away.

● **ARE YOU over 6 foot tall,** well-built, alert, keen, with a smart mind, a good education and think you deserve a better opportunity in the world today? Cocky little bugger aren't you.

● **SURPRISE YOUR FRIENDS.** Burn their houses down. **The British League of Arsonists** needs urgent help.

● **Ex**-Submarine Commander's Sailors. Contact Michael or Bernie, Portsmouth. **BOX 1.**

3rd nymphomaniac girl required to share student mini-bus to Cairo. **No middle class.** Dead Butch Adventure Tours Ltd, Earls Court Road.

● **WELSH DRESSER** for disposal. Ex-BBC. Would share digs with ex-theatrical. **Ring Benny the Bent, Porthcawl 2000.**

● **FOR SALE.** Ex-Submarine Commander's U-Boat. Contact Admiral A. Doenitz. Would part exchange for caravan in North Wales.

GENUINE NEW
SOLID LEATHER

ARMY BOOTS

ALL SIZES 4 to 12. Black only. (Size 11 is without Toecaps.) For tough hard wear and comfort. Solid leather soles.
Supple leather uppers. Steel tips on heel.

£2.65 P/P 25p

● **FOR YOU AT 65!** A dozen haddocks. **Write NOW to:** The Imperial Consolidated But Rather Fish-Orientated Insurance Co.

● **SEND NO MONEY** to the Extremely Poor Society.

● **NEW MEMBERS** urgently required for **Suicide Club,** Watford area.

● **PERSONAL VIBRATORS,** no batteries. No fuss. Very little mess. I HAVE by chance inherited a lorry load of good whisky. Reasonable offers to **Brian Schtum, BOX 439. AS SEEN ON TELEVISION.** (Police Five, Sept. 1971)

● **DO YOU SUFFER FROM** upset stomach, bad breath, poor digestion, heartburn, heat rash and indigestion? **Eurgh.**

● **EX GOURDONSTOUN** Public Schoolboy, Cambridge degree in History, **Slight Welsh speaking,** own driving licence. Seeks lucrative employment in **the Pall Mall area. Anything considered.** Contact Box P.O.W. or ring Buckghm Plce after 6 p.m.

● **PERSONAL PRODUCTS.** Manufacturers of **creams, jellies** & sweeties. You may have heard of a product and been too shy to ask for it. Serves you right you pathetic dirty-minded little weed.

● **WELSHMAN** will exchange 1927 mint condition bronze halfpenny for one exactly the same. **Pointless Swaps Ltd, Swansea.**

● **IN LOVING MEMORY OF TONY.** Dropped by the RAF over Hamburg. "Still ne'mind, eh?" Longfellow.

THIS is the genuine ENGLISH GLENDON EASI-SUIT.

You can spill food on it . . .
You can get mud on it . . .
You can pour oil on it . . .
But it'll ruin it.

Sizes AA, RAC, BBC only.

TERYLENE/WORSTED SUIT LENGTHS

DIRECT FROM THE MILL

● **Unwanted** pregnancy tests – K. Rahmin, 28, Line St., E.7

Juliette

KEN SHABBY & ROSEMAR
a true love story of our times

Ken Shabby and Rosemary have fallen violently in love.

Ken proposes marriage to Rosemary. Blissfully she agrees.

Rosemary's father finds Ken and Rosema together in his lovely home.

Ken announces that he wishes to marry Rosemary because he hasn't had it in weeks.

Rosemary's father suggests the Abbey.

True love prevails.

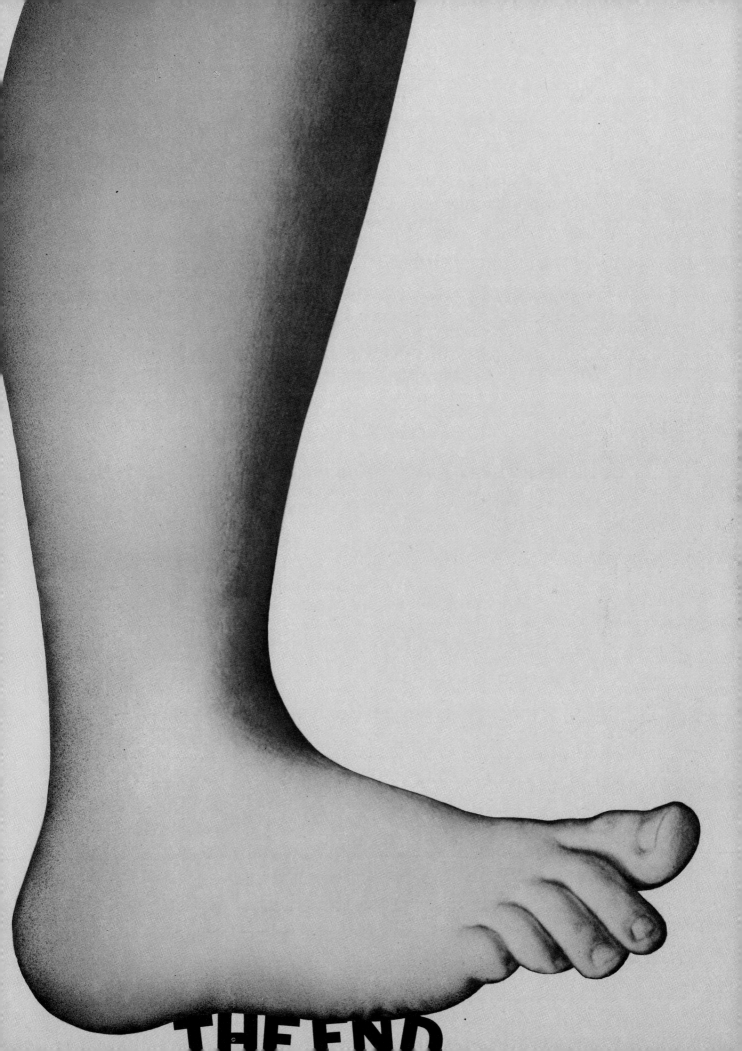

THE END

THE END

**MONTY PYTHON'S BIG BROWN BOOK
was brought to you by the makers of:**

**(in a rather silly order) Michael Palin, Eric Idle,
Graham Chapman, Terry Jones, John Cleese and the
Illustrated Terry Gilliam**

It was edited by Eric Idle

**Photographed by Doug Webb, BBC News Picture Library,
The Radio Times, Hulton Picture Library, John Horton, Tony Sullivan**

**Art Directed by Derek Birdsall
(from the North of England)**

**Art Edited and lay-outed by Katy Hepburn
(from the South of England)**

Artworked by Roger Hudson & Stephen Scales

Music arranged by Fred Tomlinson

Fights arranged by Ian McNaughton

**Gowns by Jean Louis
Mr. Cleese's wig by Maxwell of Bond St**

Mr. Bosanquet's photograph by Ian Vaughan

Thanks are due to: BBC, ITN, Kettledrum Productions

Money is due to: Reginald Bosanquet

**The Book is dedicated to BBC Programme Planners, without
whom anything is possible**

The authors are anxious to get in touch with compliant ladies under
25 with large breasts, or anybody who just likes authors.

Why Accountancy is not boring

WHY ACCOUNTANCY IS NOT BORING by Mr. A. Putey

First let me say how very pleased I was to be asked on the 14th inst. to write an article on why accountancy is not boring. I feel very very strongly that there are many people who may think that accountancy *is* boring, but they would be wrong, for it is not at all boring, as I hope to show you in this article, which is, as I intimated earlier, a pleasure to write.

I think I can do little worse than begin this article by describing why accountancy is *not* boring as far as *I* am concerned, and then, perhaps, go on to a more general discussion of why accountancy as a whole is not boring. As soon as I awake in the morning it is not boring. I get up at 7.16, and my wife Irene, an ex-schoolteacher, gets up shortly afterwards at 7.22. Breakfast is far from boring, and soon I am ready to leave the house. Irene, a keen Rotarian, hands me my briefcase and rolled umbrella at 7.53, and I leave the house seconds later. It is a short walk to Sutton station, but by no means a boring one. There is so much to see, including Mr Edgeworth, who also works at Robinson Partners. Mr Edgeworth is an extremely interesting man, and was in Uxbridge during the war. Then there is a train journey of 22 minutes to London Bridge, one of British Rail's main London termini, where we accountants mingle for a moment with stockbrokers and other accountants from all walks of life. I think that many of the people to whom accountancy appears boring think that all accountants are the same. Nothing could be further from the truth. Some accountants are chartered, but very many others are certified. I am a certified accountant, as indeed is Mr Edgeworth, whom I told you about earlier. However, in the next office to mine is a Mr Manners, who is a chartered accountant, and, incidentally, a keen Rotarian. However, Mr Edgeworth and I get on extremely well with Mr Manners, despite the slight prestige superiority of his position. Mr Edgeworth, in fact, gets on with Mr Manners extremely well, and if there are two spaces at lunch it is more than likely he will sit with Mr Manners. So far, as you can see, accountancy is not boring. During the morning there are a hundred and one things to do. A secretary may pop in with details of an urgent audit. This happened in 1967 and again last year. On the other hand, the phone may ring, or there may be details of a new superannuation scheme to mull over. The time flies by in this not at all boring way, and it is soon 10.00, when there is only 1 hour to go before Mrs Jackson brings round the tea urn. Mrs Jackson is just one of the many people involved in accountancy who give the lie to those who say it is a boring profession. Even a solicitor or a surveyor would find Mrs Jackson a most interesting person. At 11.05, having drunk an interesting cup of tea, I put my cup on the tray and then...

(18 pages deleted here – Ed.) .. and once the light is turned out by Irene, a very keen Rotarian, I am left to think about how extremely un-boring my day has been, being an accountant. Finally may I say how extremely grateful I am to your book for so generously allowing me so much space. (Sorry, Putey! – Ed.)

PAGE SEVENTEEN

Well, hello and welcome to page seventeen. In many books, page 17 is a sad anti-climax after the exciting events described on pages 15 and 16. We hope to avoid this pitfall by making our page 17 into one of the most exciting and action-packed page 17s that you've ever read. In a lot of books, page 17 contains purely descriptive matter, and in others it is still only part of the introduction, but not so this one. . . . We say: get a move on, novelists! and let's have more page 17s like this one:

> of her dress as it rode up over her thighs, her slender body thrust forward by the enormous power of the 6,000h.p. engines, as Horst hurled the car into a shrieking, sickening slide across the wet tarmac. The lion tore savagely at his bronzed thighs as the car soared into the air, turned, twisted, and plunged down the treacherous ski slope, that no man had ever survived. Tenderly Eunice caressed him as the fighters screeched out of the darkness, flames ripping towards him. The sea was coming nearer and nearer, and though neither had eaten for eight weeks, the stark terror of what they saw, gave them the last drop of energy to push their bodies to the limits. Eunice groaned, the dark figure of Shahn-el-Shid, dagger raised, hurled himself from the sheer wall of the palace. Horst reversed, swerved, coughed and threw himself into the gorge. Never had Horst known such exquisite pleasure, as far above him a million Dervishes swept into the fort, looting and pillaging. The Colonel screamed an order, and with one enormous blast the refinery was a sheet of flame – a wall of fire six miles long and eight miles high. Eunice groaned as the spacecraft roared low over the silent, darkened surface of this eerie world, a million light years from the Earth they had left only seconds before, a planet doomed to extinction, when suddenly
>
> 17

How about that for a page 17? Wake up Dickens! Wake up Graham Greene! Let's show the World that British literature gets on with it!

Naughty pages

Rip off the
naughty parts.

Biofit Cleans Whiter than Acid

These are the understains. The biological stains we get from our bodies. The filthy unpleasant stains you get from simply living. The nasty putrescent beastly excreted stains you can't mention. The foul pestilential ugly horrific smells and stains which come from every day life. The corpusculent puss-filled emanations, the plaguey, ulcerous, febrile deposits and stains that come from normal living. The nasty, contagious, nauseating, pyretic infections, the purulent festering, cankerous malignant vile running poisons and stains – oh I love them. I love them.

Join the professionals

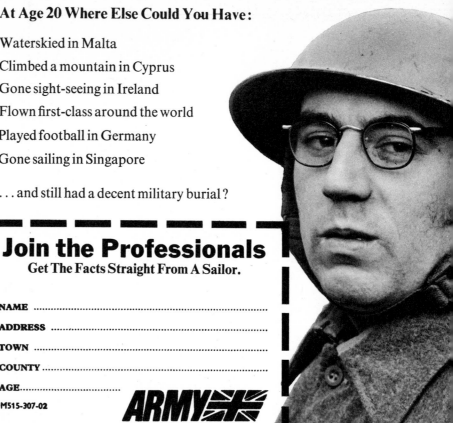

At Age 20 Where Else Could You Have:

Waterskied in Malta

Climbed a mountain in Cyprus

Gone sight-seeing in Ireland

Flown first-class around the world

Played football in Germany

Gone sailing in Singapore

. . . and still had a decent military burial?

VOTE WISELY
VOTE SILLY

THE SILLY PARTY

The leader of the Silly Party
The Rt. Hon. Loopy X

Support the Silly Party. The only party
that is publicly committed to:

* raising prices
* destroying industry
* causing inflation
* ruining the economy

A Silly Government would:

* raise the school leaving age to 43
* encourage naughtiness in high places
* maintain confidence in British
  Silliness abroad

OX

arty. He

IN-
M-

NG
T-

h for the
ce crossed
ch (which
he door).
es on Rat
esman.

Minister of

KEYHOLE FOR EXHIBITIONISTS

VOTE SIL

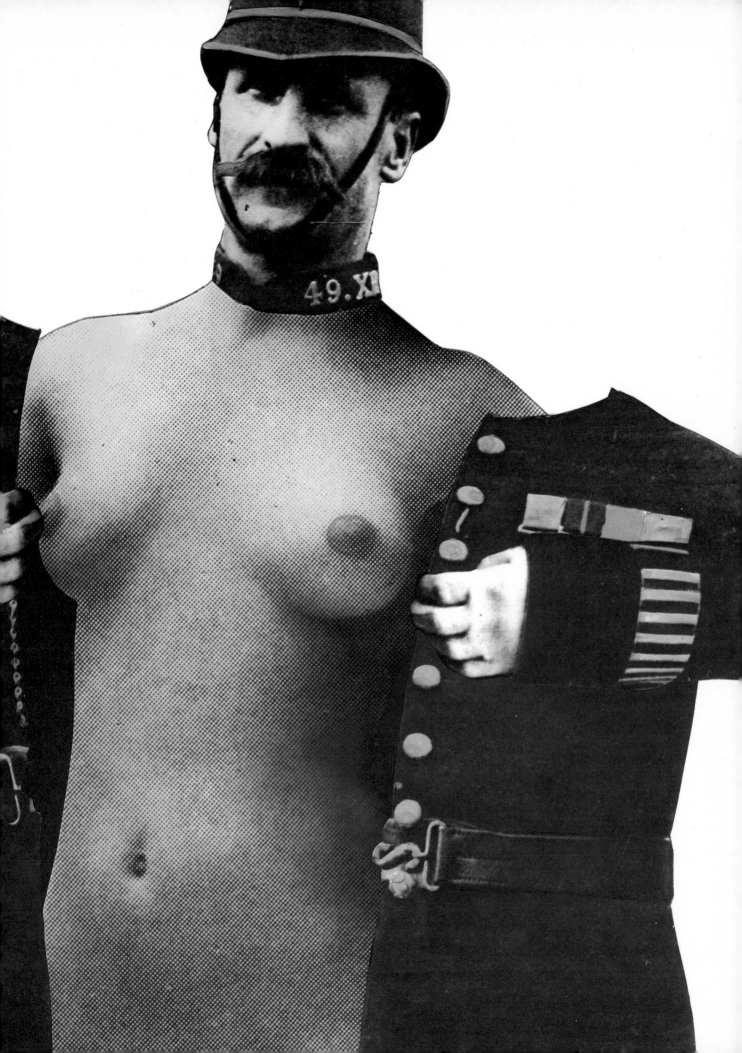

BATLEY LADIES TOWNSWOMEN'S GUILD

President: Mrs Rita Fairbanks

Mrs Fairbanks reports on this year's production

This has been a terribly good year for the Guild. Our annual production raised more than ever and was even more popular. Thanks are due to Mrs Robinson and Mrs Lowndes for doing the cakes, and of course the Vicar for the use of the field. We were the first Townswomen's Guild to put on "Camp on Blood Island" and last year of course we did our extremely popular re-enactment of "Nazi War Atrocities," so this year we decided to do something in a lighter vein. Happily we fell on "The Battle of Pearl Harbour." To all involved many thanks and let's hope that next year's production of "Groupie" will be even more successful.

Yours Truly,

Rita Fairbanks

Mrs Rita Fairbanks
The Dimples,
Bottomleigh,
Wainscotting,
Nr. Batley.

A scene from this year's product—

Mrs Rita Fairbanks and friends

y the Batley Ladies Townswomen's Guild

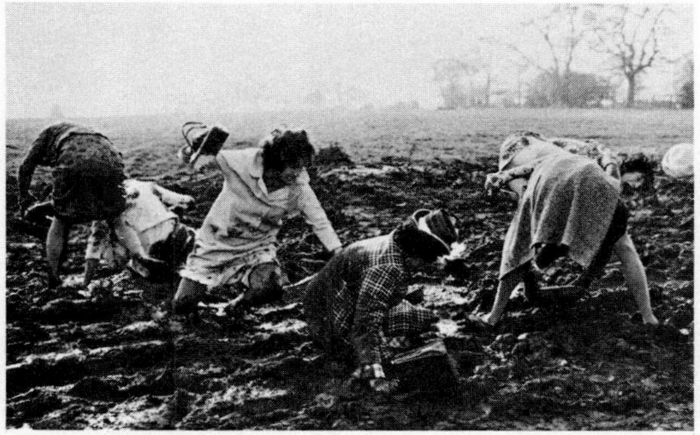

1970 Nazi War Atrocities

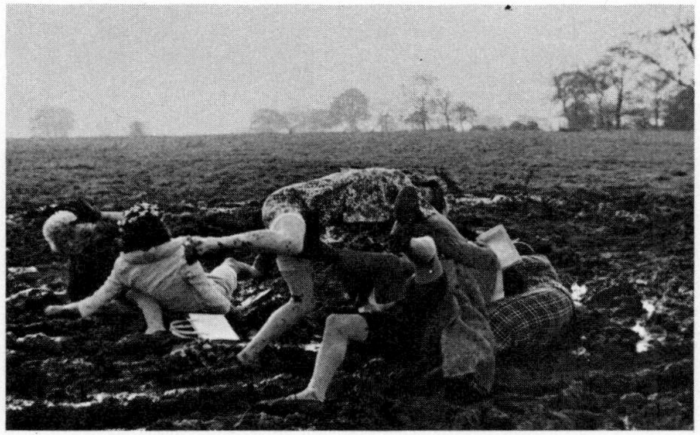

1969 Iolanthe

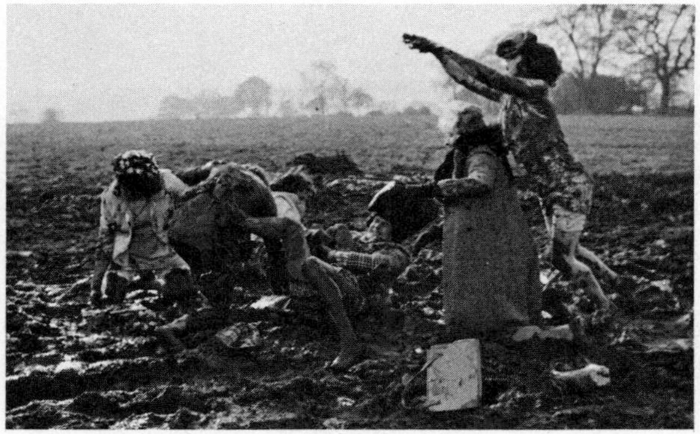

1968 Camp on Blood Island

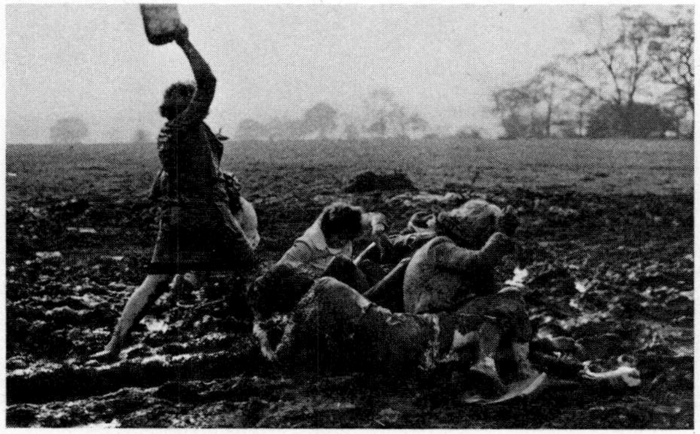

1967 A Bond Honoured

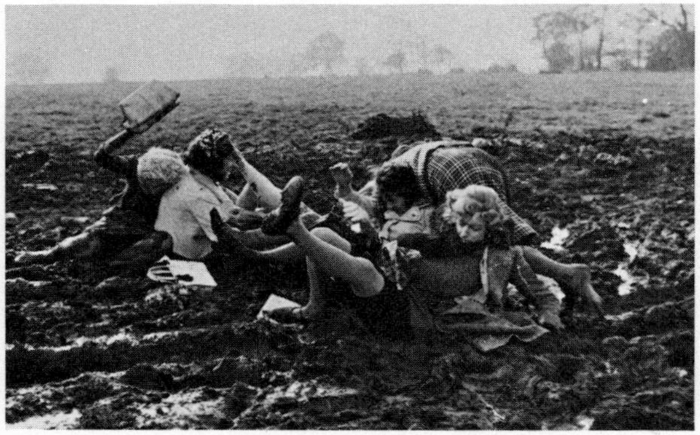

1966 Look Back in Anger

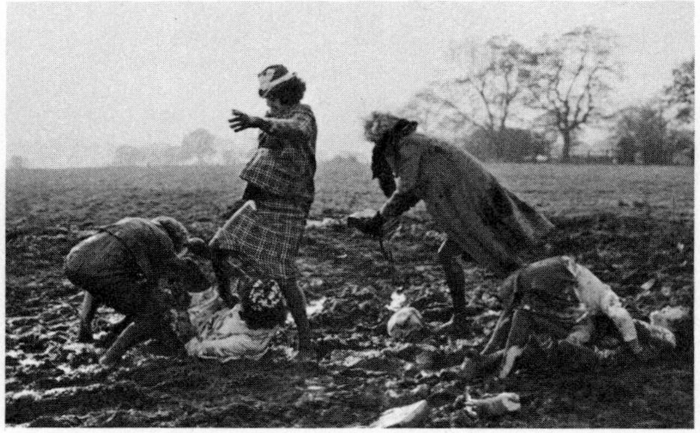

1965 The Marquis de Sade's Memoirs

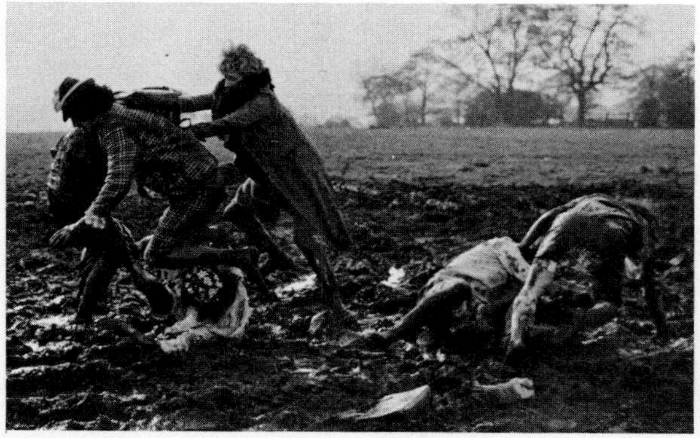

1964 The Merchant of Venice

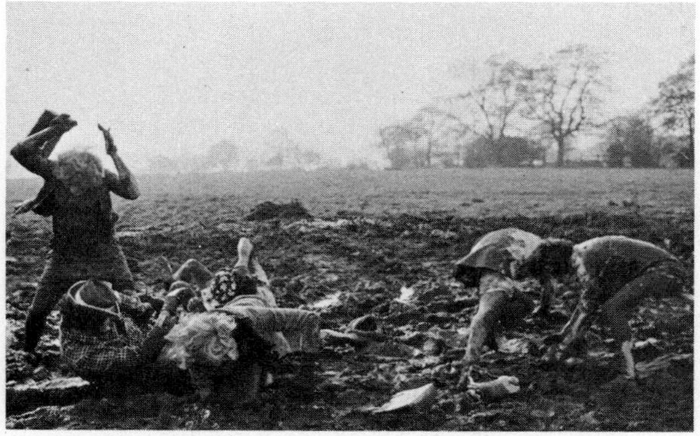

1943 The Importance of Being Earnest

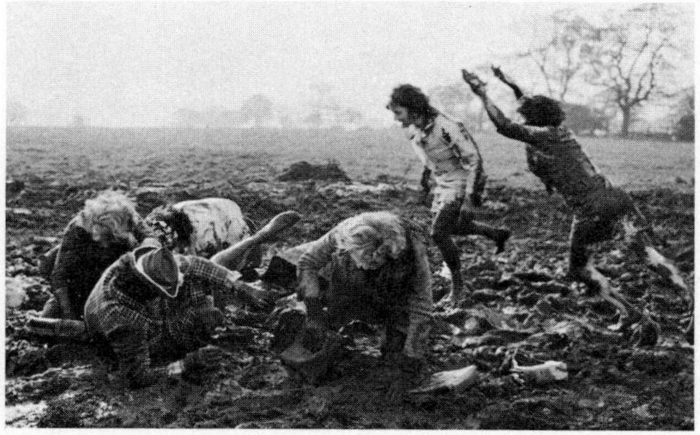

1940 Maid of the Mountains

Next year "GROUPIE"

E.D. Silly's Page

THE "ACNE" PATENT QUIZ by E. D. Silly

1. What have the following in common? a) Moshe Dayan b) Sammy Davis Jnr. c) The Nawab of Pataudi.

2. Edward Heath is a what?

3. Who wrote "The gushing leaves that through the argent windows blush?"?

4. Can you name seven planets?

5. Which of the following is not in Asia? Lahore, Singapore, Dacca, Bangkok, Coventry.

6. How many fingers am I holding up? a) 1 b) 2 c) 3 d) 46

7. What is "a hen."?
   a) a small sprochett near the tamping wopple of a Keighley trunion?
   b) a regenerative cell in the Aquarian life-support system of the Apollo Space Capsule.
   c) An egg-laying female domestic fowl.
   (Careful with this one — it might not be the obvious E.D.)

8. How do you tell a boy scout?
   a) by b) b) by c) c) in a quiet even voice so as not to frighten him until you've told him.

LLY THINGS TO DO by E. D. Silly

Take a piece of blue notepaper and stick it on the side of a chicken. Then frighten the chicken.

If you live in Birmingham, Nottingham or Leeds go: "Boinggg!"

Put a chair in the front garden and put a television on it.

Buy a packet of winegums and leave them outside Buckingham Palace.

If you have a French *au pair* staying with you, get a piece of string about 3 yards long, tie one end to your finger and let the rest trail along the ground.

If you bank with Lloyds, go to see the Manager on Jan. 4th 1972, and talk in a very high voice.

LLY THINGS TO DO ON A RAINY AFTERNOON
Stand out in the rain.

LLY GAMES by E. D. Silly

4 or more players sit round in a circle. The player nearest the one next to him deals. Whilst the deal is going on the other players have to impersonate either General Franco or any member of the P.L.F. (Palestine Liberation Front).
Each player has 7 cards, apart from the eldest one who has 9 and the other 3, who have 6. Then the player nearest the one who last went to the lavatory runs out of the room, taking his cards with him and goes to see a film. The next player must either go and see the film as well or, if he has a Jack, Queen or King of any *Black* suit, he must go to the pub. The 2 remaining players can either go to the pub or go to see a film.
The Winner is the one nearest the mantelpiece.

The Francis Of Assisi Game
The player pretending to be Francis of Assisi deals 6 cards to each player. They all then see who can remain motionless longest. The first player to move then becomes Francis of Assisi.

Drabble. A word game for 2 to 4 players. The four players sit from left to right and the first person to write a novel wins.

QUICK CROSSWORD by E. D. Silly

ACROSS
1. O Spoils! (1,6)
2. Dark bird (4,4)
3. Ant at bay (3,2,3)
4. Nor (3)
5. Grime (5)
6. Rank (4)
7. Hole (4)
8. London Philharmonic Orchestra (1,1,1)

DOWN
1. Old range (3,5)
2. Spa (3)
3. Pork trip (4,4)
4. In bather (2,6)
5. Sir talon (3,5)
6. B.O. (1,1)
7. Ye (2)

UP
1. Ron (3)

SPAM

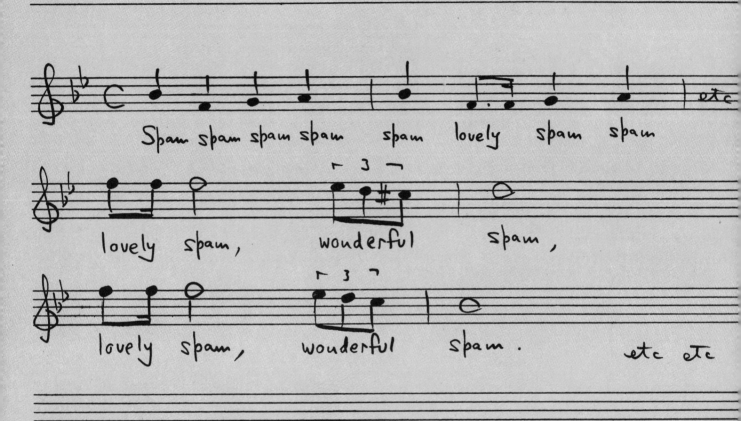

Spam spam spam spam   spam   lovely   spam   spam

lovely spam,   wonderful   spam,

lovely spam,   wonderful   spam.   etc etc

1   Spam, spam, spam, lovely spam,
    Wonderful spam, lovely spam.

    Spam, spam, spam, spam,
    Spam, spam, spam, spam, (etc)

2   Spam, spam, spam, magnificent spam,
    Superlative spam.

    Spam, spam, spam, spam,
    Spam, spam, spam, spam, (etc)

3   Spam, spam, spam, wonderous spam,
    Surgical spam, splendiferous spam.

    Spam, spam, spam, spam,
    Spam, spam, spam, spam, (etc)

Sports Page

CAPTAIN'S PAGE
IT'S JARROW DAY

TONIGHT its the Jimmy Buzzard Story (as told to Corbett Woodall)

Well Brian. Quite frankly Brian. I mean, blimey. Quite frankly Brian. I'm choked. Very choked. Pardon? Oh. Well Brian. Quite frankly Brian. What was that again? Oh. Yeah. Well Brian. Frankly Brian. I hit the ball first time and there it was in the back of the net. Thank you Brian. I'm opening a boutique.

Jimmy Buzzard in conversation with A. S. Byatt.

The rags to riches success story of Jimmy Buzzard

Bought from Hounslow Reserves by Biggleswade £15. Free Transfer to Scunthorpe. (Rail Fare: £1.50p.) Dramatic midnight signing in a club in Soho. Jimmy goes to Inter-Milan for £3 (and the lady's expenses).

Cycles back. Plays for Under 23's against the Over 40's at Doncaster. Catches the eye of Jarrow Manager Syd "Hammerhead" Hawkins on a London Weekend Late-Night Revue Show. Signs on for £20 and four light and bitters to become part of the now legendary Jarrow forward line of Bunn, Whackett, Buzzard, Stubble and Boot. Scores the winning goal in the second half of the 3rd Round, First Leg, Inter-European Playoff Competition against A.C. Finland. Granted the freedom of Jarrow.

Brian Thigh writes

The Limpid eloquence of this surely tactile abstract expressionist of the football field lies in his Kantian positivism, his Cézanne-like use of positioning, and his almost Proustian ability to head the ball into the net. "Mais où sont les neiges d'antan" Buzzard might well have been thinking as he rammed the ball eloquently into the by now out-argued Finnish goal. It was an assertion of manhood, a reassurance of spring, a cunning restatement of Cartier's rebirth theory, above all it was offside. Still such niceties have never bothered master-

The big fight

Already its been dubbed "Fight of the fortnight."

KEN CLEAN-AIR SYSTEM
Height	6 foot 5
Weight	15 stone
Reach	36 inches
Inside leg	34 inches
Previous fights	24

ELAINE GRIFFITHS
Height	5 foot
Weight	7 stone
Reach	25 inches
Inside leg	24 inches
Previous fights	none

Ken is interested in gravel, and collects housebricks. Elaine is a southpaw and is keen on Cliff Richard records.

Can Ken do it?
by A. PUNDIT

The great white hope of British boxing takes to the ring tonight with a record of 24 fights and only three convictions. He's fighting fit again now that an operation has removed the small particle of brain that was lodged in his skull. Dubbed "invincible" by his mother, each morning now for several months Ken has got up at 3 a.m. to jog the 15 miles from his 2 bedroomed, 6 bathroomed, 4 up, 2 down, 3 to go luxury house in Reigate to the Government's Pesticide Research Centre at Shoreham. Nobody knows why. Tonight he takes on Elaine Griffiths, the plucky little Birmingham schoolgirl who's just turned professional after one amateur fight. (A draw against Myra Robinson). Can Ken do it? Personally I think

Ken Clean-air System V Elaine Griffiths

butcher Len Pastry who unhesitatingly awarded the winning goal.

I for one shall never forget that magic moment in the 82nd minute when skipper Nobby Boot ran fully forty yards in the mud through a packed Finnish defence to kiss Jimmy Buzzard full on the lips after he'd scored. This surely is what football is all about?

he can. I think Ken has the experience and the know-how to batter this young schoolgirl to the ground in a bloody pulp within ten rounds to give British Boxing the shot in the arm I so badly need.

Pictured at the weigh-in for tonights Big fight.

Norman Mailer Himself on the big fight

Norman Mailer writes about his ego

Tonight Ken will be swimming down subterranean rivers of exhaustion, staring at the light of his own death in the self-fulfilling process of his ego-consciousness, travelling the crossroads of karma, past the yawning appeals of the swooning catacombs of oblivion, experiencing the psychologically incomprehensible, the ultimately immense incommunicable oneness of a thousand dollars a paragraph, syndicated with repeats.

Norman Mailer will be Resumed as Soon as Possible.

Arts Page

Shunt's Utopia

Gavin Millarrrrrrrrrr writes:

Neville Shunt's latest West End Success – *It All Happened on the 11.20 from Hainault to Redhill via Horsham and Reigate, calling at Carshalton Beeches, Malmesbury, Tooting Bec and Croydon West* is currently appearing at the Limp Theatre, Piccadilly. What Shunt is doing in this, as in his earlier nine plays, is to express the human condition in terms of British Rail.

Some people have made the mistake of seeing Shunt's work as a load of rubbish about railway timetables, but clever people like me who talk loudly in restaurants see this as a deliberate ambiguity, a plea for understanding in a mechanised mansion. The points are frozen, the beast is dead. What is the difference? What indeed is the point? The point is frozen, the beast is late out of Paddington. The point is taken. If La Fontaine's elk would spurn Tom Jones the engine must be our head, the dining car our oesophagus, the guards van our left lung, the cattle truck our shins, the first class compartment the piece of skin at the nape of the neck and the level crossing an electric elk called Simon. The clarity is devastating. But where is the ambiguity? Over there in a box. Shunt is saying the 8.15 from Gillingham when in reality he means the 8.13 from Gillingham. The train is the same, only the time is altered. Ecce homo, ergo elk. La Fontaine knew its sister and knew her bloody well. The point is taken, the beast is moulting, the fluff gets up your nose. The illusion is complete; it is reality, the reality is illusion and the ambiguity is the only truth. But is the truth, as Hitchcock observes, in the box? No, there isn't room, the ambiguity has put on weight. The point is taken, the elk is dead, the beast stops at Swindon, Chabrol stops at nothing, I'm having treatment and La Fontaine can get knotted.

Gavin Millarrrrrrrrrrrrr wrrrrrrrrrrrote

How to make films

by Fellini in conversation with Mrs Rodgers

MRS RODGERS: What do you want?
FELLINI: I am a leading Italian film director, can I come in?
MRS RODGERS: What for?
FELLINI: I want to talk to you about my work.
MRS RODGERS: Are you from the brickworks?
FELLINI: No! No! I'm a film director.
MRS RODGERS: They're all bloody wops at the brickworks.
LOSEY: Madam, I can vouch for my friend here. He is one of the greatest modern film directors, surely you've heard of *Giulietta Degli Spiriti*?
MRS RODGERS: Go away.
FELLINI: We just want to talk about film-making.
MRS RODGERS: Well, I haven't got time to sit and natter, I've got me husband's tea to get ready.
AGNES VARDA: Madame Rodgers, réalisez-vous l'importance de ce directeur ici?
MRS RODGERS: What's she on about?
LOSEY: Do you feel that Fellini's work relies too heavily on symbolism and ritual?
MRS RODGERS: Shove off, or I'll call the police.
CASSAVETES: Great!

Next week: Kurosawa talks to Mrs Lewis at the Co-op

Port Shoem by The Speverent Roone

I've a Gouse and Harden in the country
An ace I call my plown,
A treat I can replace to
When I beed to knee alone.
Catterfly and butterpillar
Perch on beefy lough
And I listen to the dats and cogs
As they mark and they biaow.
Yes wature here is nunderful
There is no weed for nords,
While silling by my windowflutter
Biny little tirds.

Short Poem

Po.

Horace Poem

Horace

*Much to his Mum and Dad's dismay
Horace ate himself one day.
He didn't stop to say his grace,
He just sat down and ate his face.
"We can't have this!" his Dad declared,
"If that lad's ate, he should be shared."
But even as he spoke they saw
Horace eating more and more:
First his legs and then his thighs,
His arms, his nose, his hair, his eyes . . .
"Stop him someone!" Mother cried
"Those eyeballs would be better fried!"
But all too late, for they were gone,
And he had started on his dong . . .
"Oh! foolish child!" the father mourns
"You could have deep-fried that with prawns,
Some parsley and some tartar sauce . . ."
But H. was on his second course:
His liver and his lights and lung,
His ears, his neck, his chin, his tongue;
"To think I raised him from the cot
And now he's going to scoff the lot!"
His Mother cried: "What shall we do?
What's left won't even make a stew . . ."
And as she wept, her son was seen
To eat his head, his heart, his spleen.
And there he lay: a boy no more,
Just a stomach, on the floor . . .
None the less, since it was his
They ate it – that's what haggis is.**

**No it isn't. Ed. Haggis is a kind of stuffed black pudding
eaten by the Scots and considered by them to be not only a
delicacy but fit for human consumption. The minced
heart, liver and lungs of a sheep, calf or other animal's
inner organs are mixed with oatmeal, sealed and boiled
in maw in the sheep's intestinal stomach-bag and . . .
Excuse me a minute. Ed.*

THE WORLD ENCYCLOPAEDI

The World Encyclopaedia of Carnal Knowledge
published in Nice weekly parts by

Purves Press Ltd
New Solicitors Letter Lane
EC1

Coming soon*
FIND OUT ABOUT YOURSELF, FIND OUT ABOUT YOUR FRIENDS, FIND OUT ABOUT THEIR BODIES!

* See issue 13 for remedies

Did you know that a nude lady looks like this?

(Published by permission of the National Hospital, the British Museum, Nobby, Vera and Sam Ltd.)

The World Encyclopaedia of Carnal Knowledge will be out soon.
It will show you what a nude lady looks like. (Incidentally she looks like this –)

It is bursting with information
* Did you know that a woman can have as many as 14 orgasms during one telephone call?
* Did you know that a man's penis can also be used for peeing?
* Did you know that a woman looks like this naked?

How to have fun
When to have fun
Where to have fun
Europe on Five Women a Day
　　　　　by A. Doctor.

It will contain pages and pages packed with information and pictures of your body and the bodies of lovely ladies.
Teach yourself everything comes complete with diagrams and cut-out feet.
positions:

No. 37.

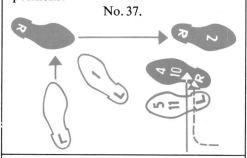

QUIZ
WHAT DO YOU KNOW ABOUT YOUR BODY?
1. Varicose veins can be fun at parties. a) true; b) false.
2. If there was an outbreak of rubella at your local school you'd be worried because it was: a) german measles; b) chicken pox; c) mumps; d) contagious.
3. At what age should a child be able to make up a simple sentence? a) 18 months; b) 14 years; c) 37 years.
4. Julius Caesar was the first: a) Caesarian birth; b) Roman pouff; c) Doctor.
5. Your clavicle is: a) your collar bone; b) your harpsichord; c) your au pair girl.
6. How many pints does your body contain? a) between eight and ten; b) between ten and midnight; c) four double gins; d) a bottle of whisky.
7. If you burnt your hand cooking the best thing to do would be: a) stop cooking; b) eat out; c) put a plaster on it; d) get pissed.
8. A woman's breasts contain: a) milk; b) fun; c) naughty secrets.
9. If a man put his hand on your encyclopaedia you'd: a) have a fit; b) have a nice time; c) have a disease.
10. Nymphomaniacs should be: a) encouraged; b) put in hospitals; c) fuckx
borxx

BALPA SPOKESMAN

We in the British Airline Pilots Asso tion can thoroughly recommend handy encyclopaedia. Incidentally I w little bit upset that I wasn't asked to v the Foreword to the whole book, it's just itinerant newsreaders who can do job you know. Sorry about this little b irrelevance in what is after all just a s line recommendation on a totally diffe subject. Still, these things need saying. (No they don't. Ed.)

Improve your fun by sending away for special equipment, the ropes, the climb frame and the trampoline.
PLUS exciting free gifts.
Issue Two:

A rubber bath mat.

Now you need no longer be ashamed of secrets of your body *
For example, did you know that a na lady looks like this?

*Unless it's a particularly nasty one.

YOUR PROBLEMS BY A. DOCTOR

Mrs Stibart of Woking:
No, this most certainly never happens.
...t you have been told is an old wives'
... about Mrs Dennis Snowden, 12 The
...ons, Notlob, and the trouble she had
...her younger Michael and their cousin
...y Davis (who was soon to become quite
...known). Anyway, suddenly Middle
...hael attacked Youngest Michael with
...labrador and before Mrs Snowden
...d stop her, plucky young Betty pulled
...e dog's fur off.
...Living with a nude dog would not have
...ed Mrs Snowden's neuralgia or pain in
...umbar region.

Yours sincerely,
A. Doctor.

...r Doctor,
...Could you describe to me the politi-
...state of Europe in those final years
...re the start of the 1914–18 War?

Yours,
Mrs Etc.

...r Mrs. Etcetera,
My post bag is full – week after week
...letters asking me about this very same
...lem. Well, I have consulted many of my
...ical colleagues on this vexed question,
...I'm afraid that all we've been able to
...e up with is that on 28th June 1914ish –
...z Ferdinand, we think it was, although
...rofessor of gynaecology at King's
...ege Hospital, thought it was Mrs
...xander Graham Bell, who incidentally
...quite a lot of trouble with her womb,
...t to the Bosnian Capital of Sarajevo,
...was assassinated there by Bosnians.
...dentally, Archduke Ferdinand had quite
...t of trouble with his varicose veins
...'s later years which of course nowadays
...ess of a problem with improved surgical
...kings, injections and of course the
...ations, which I told you of in my letter
...t the Boxer Rebellion.

...ald,
There is absolutely no cause for
...ern – your 'habit' as you call it, is
...lutely normal and can cause none of the
...ors of which you speak, and is in no way
...imental to your health. But of course, if
...lged in to excess, will be even more fun.

...ifer of Sudbury,
Of course these are not rodents, but if
...are worried about it cover yourself
...ally with RID-A-WEASEL-STOAT-
...T-MOUSE-RABBITEX and I'm sure
...ll have no further trouble in the region
...mentioned. (Although maybe still in the
...ningham region.)

Dear Doctor,
I am writing to you because I have begun to be worried about being covered with enormous boils and warts. They have now completely covered the entire surface of my body except the little bits in between my toes, which are at the moment on loan from the man at number 17. Were it not for these bits I would be at the end of my tether.

Yours sincerely,
James Sutcliffe.
P.S. Sorry about the pus on the paper.

Dear Mr. Sutcliffe,
There is absolutely nothing for you to worry about, except of course that your rent is overdue, and if I do not receive the sum within 7 days, bailliffs will come round and duff you up A TREAT. I am writing this to you personally rather than publish it in my column because I am a kind man in that I have not called round to press your eyeballs in – yet.

Yours in anticipation,
A. Doctor.

For legal reasons this letter is in no way published. I didn't put it in. Ed.

Features include
Why wear Clothes? Yes or No? Is Nudity Really Fun? Why Not? Should We All be Naked? Shall We or Shan't We? Why Not be Bare? Should We or Shouldn't We? Might We as Well Drop 'em? Oh All Right Then.

Contributors include M. Drabble, D. Nimmo, M. T. Tung, C. Guevara, A. Hayden Jones & Her Husband Pip, The Amazing Kargol and Janet.

Articles include Wife Swapping. Do Sex Magazines Sell? Does it Really Make You Blind? Bodily Hair; Yes, No or Conservative. How to Avoid Unwanted Articles.

PLUS The Consumer's Guide to Hospitals including
St. Rumour's Hospital for Pretty Rich Girls With Nothing Particularly Wrong with Them
The Brixton Nasties Clinic
The Royal Free Hospital for Dead People
The Royal Rich Hospital for People who like Nurses Who are Real Goers and No Questions Asked

Issue One; The Henry Cooper Hospital

Wrestling

Boxing

---

1. Sex test
Do you really like sex?
a) No
b) Yes
c) What is your address?

2. Colour blindness test
How many colours can you see in the following:

27: Normal
1: You're colour blind
None: You're blind

3. Proclivity test
Are you normal?
a) Do you like going out with men?
b) Are you a man?
c) What are you doing on Saturday?

4. Did you know several naked ladies look like this?

HOW YOUR BODY WORKS by A. NOTHER DOCTOR

The human body is indeed a wonderful thing. Its infinitely complex way of functioning would take a computer, working flat out, day and night, excluding Bank Holidays and Christmas, 3,971 years to work out. The slightest flicker of the eyelid, the smallest movement of the big toe involves such extraordinarily complex processes that the average man, working flat out, excluding Bank Holidays and Christmas, but *including* weekends would take 84,643 light years to work it out. If you can imagine an Airedale terrier jumping in and out of a watering can once every 7 minutes for 12 years you have some idea how long that would take. And that's only one light year.

Even the most simple process that the body can perform – like paying the doctor – would take a piece of asbestos over 9 billion years to work out. If you can imagine a man at a cocktail party congratulating the hostess on the avocado dip 40,000 times every second for $2\frac{1}{2}$ hours twice a week for 28,000 years you can begin to realise what an extraordinarily wonderful thing the human body is.

To put it even more simply, if you can imagine a doctor leaving his lucrative Harley St. practice to a younger partner, and cruising round the world 4 times a year, drinking 3 bottles of champagne with a friend's wife every afternoon, and writing an article on How Your Body Works once every 96 days, you'll get some idea of why I was struck off the register. Good evening.

Australian Page

AN AUSTRALIAN LAMENT

Australia's a lovely land
It's full of bonza blokes,
Sheilas, beer and no-one's queer
Except in Pommie jokes.

Australians are lovely chaps
They're God's own chosen race.
If they ever see a fairy Pom
They'll smash him in the face.

Australians like dressing up
In skirts and having fun
And that's all we were doing
When the Vice Squad came along.

Q : What is the ideal wife for an Australian?
A : A dumb, rich nymphomaniac who owns a pub.

This here's the wattle
The emblem of our land
You can stick it in a bottle
Or you can hold it in your hand.

Children's Page

Hello children hello. This is Uncle Dennis welcoming you to your own page. Hello. Today we are going to have a story, so sit comfortably and we can all start.

One day, Rikki the magic Pixie, went to visit Daisy Bumble in her tumbledown cottage. He found her in the bedroom. Roughly he grabbed her heaving shoulders pulling her down on to the bed and hurriedly ripping off her thin ████████████████

Old Nick, the Sea Captain was a rough tough jolly sort of fellow. He loved the life of the sea and he loved to hang out down by the pier where the men dressed as ladies████████ ████████████████████ with a melon.

Rumpletweezer ran the Dinky Tinky shop in the foot of the Magic oak tree by the wobbly dum dum tree in the shade of the magic glade down in Dingly Dell. Here he sold contraceptives, ████████████ and various appliances ████████████ naked fun ████████ f████████ ████████ sh██ ████████

Herbert Anchny invites you to play....

POSTAL
BLACKMAIL

BLACKMA

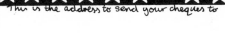

This is the address to send your cheques to

Blackmail,
Behind the hot water pipes,
Third washroom along,
Victoria Station.

£40

This is the mistress of a well known Banker in Hounslow.

That's £40 please to stop us revealing your name Mr. X, so that your wife Doreen, and your lovely children Diane, Janice and Juliet need never know the name of your mistress in Hounslow.

£3000

This is the first of a series of photographs which could add up to a divorce, premature retirement and possible criminal proceedings for a Company Director in Bromsgrove. So Mr. S. £3000 please to stop us revealing:

a) Whose shoulders you are sitting on
b) What you are doing
c) The names of the three people involved
d) The youth organisation to which they belong
e) And the shop where you bought the equipment

£100

We'll be showing you more of this photograph unless we hear from Charles or Michael.

TONIGHT'S STAR PRIZE

£5000

Who is the Star?

He's a well known singer.
He sings mainly ballads.
He does a lot of youth work.

FOR £350

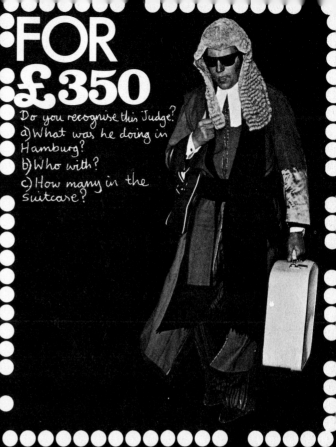

Do you recognise this Judge?
a) What was he doing in Hamburg?
b) Who with?
c) How many in the suitcase?

£1000

OR
Win a short service commission in the Gay Gordons

Take a good look at these soldiers.
Which regiment are they?
Who is their Commanding Officer?
1) Is he? 2) Did he?
3) Does he
4) Should he?

This is the Headmaster of a prominent Public School. So Mr. P of S. this is your last chance to pay, otherwise your lovely Board of Governors will be receiving your name, your costumes, and the rest of the negatives.

£50

Newsreader Spot.

Can you spot the Newsreader?
Is he ITN or BBC?
Who is he with?
Which is the programme Planner?
Could he write a foreword?

A Song for Europe

"BING TIDDLE TIDDLE BONG"
THIS YEAR'S WINNER AT MONACO

Chanté par
"Les Deux Hommes Célèbres"

"BING TIDDLE TIDDLE BONG"

A SONG FOR EUROPE   *This year's winners: MONACO*   *Chanté par "Les Deux Hommes Célèbres*

Les lyrics par
LES ROBERTS

Musique composée p
BRIAN TRUBSHAW

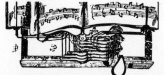

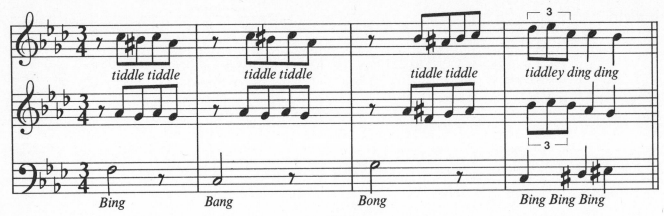

tiddle tiddle   tiddle tiddle   tiddle tiddle   tiddley ding ding

Bing   Bang   Bong   Bing Bing Bing

Les lyrics

Les intro :   *"Mais je pense...."*

Les chorus :   *Bing tiddle tiddle bang*
                 Bing tiddle tiddle bing
                 Bing tiddle tiddle tiddle tiddle
                 Bing tiddle tiddle bong

Les verse one :   *Bang tuddle tuddle bing*
                 Bung taddle taddle bong
                 Bing toddle toddle toddle toddle
                 Bong toddle toddle bing

Chorus :   *Oh, bing tiddle tiddle les etc.*

Les verse two, répétez les verse one

Chorus :   *Mais oui, bing tiddle tiddle*
                 (encore d'etcetera)

This is nine-year-old Sally Bent
who sang Britain's entry
"Bang, bang, bang, bang",
which came joint fourth.
Sally is ten and has her own
series on BBC 2.

HOW THEY FARED

First : **Monaco with "Bing tiddle tiddle Bong"**
Second : **Italy with "Si si boing bang"**
Third : **Germany with "Nein bong über tiddle"**
Equal Fourth : **England with "Bang bang bang bang"**
                Ireland with "Ay ay ay ay"
                Scotland with "Och och och och"
                Israel with "Oy oy oy oy"
Fifth : **France with "Post coitum omnia animal tristes est"**
Sixth : **Sweden with a "Ding ding a dong"**

THE IMPORTANCE OF BEING EARNEST
A New Version by Billy Bremner

Act One

Morning Room in Algernon's Flat in Half-Moon St. WI. Time: The present. The room is luxuriously and artistically furnished. The sound of a piano is heard in an adjoining room.
LANE is arranging afternoon tea on the table, and after the music has ceased ALGERNON enters.

ALGERNON: Lorimer had a great game, Don.

LANE: Yes, fantastic goal, no one could have stopped that.

ALGERNON: Mind you, I think Alan Clarke laid the ball off nicely for him.

LANE: Yes, he had a good game.

Enter "CHOPPER" HARRIS

ALGERNON: Hello, Chopper.

CHOPPER *brings* ALGERNON *down from behind.*

LANE: For God's sake, ref. did you see that, you nearly took his left leg off.

CHOPPER: I fell over.

Enter JACKIE CHARLTON

JACKIE: I'll get him.

ALGERNON: Watch out, Jackie.

Curtain

Act Two

Garden at the Manor House, Woolton. A flight of grey stone steps leads up to the house. The garden is full of roses. There are two basket chairs and a table covered with books. MISS PRISM is seated, CECILY is watering flowers. JOHNNY GILES floats in a perfect swerving corner PAUL MADELEY nods it into the net.

CECILY: Great goal, Paul.

Curtain

Act Three

The changing room at Elland Road. The air is thick with steam from the baths. Football boots and mud-stained white shirts lie discarded on the floor. Occasional shouts and splashes are heard. LADY BRACKNELL comes over from the West Ham bath.

LADY BRACKNELL: Great goal, Paul, that's what we needed.

MADELEY: Thanks, boss.

Enter "CHOPPER" HARRIS. He brings LADY BRACKNELL down with a sliding tackle and a series of short left jabs to the head.

ALGERNON: He's done it again.

CHOPPER: I slipped on the soap.

Curtain

Are you civilised?
Have you been civilised recently?

Cut out this picture of Sir Kenneth Clark and stick it in your living room window.

Le Pouff Celebre

Bonjour les hommes, et à toutes les madames bonjour encore – pas oublier les enfants, les mademoiselles, et les vendeurs de légumes vertes. Bonjour à tout le monde!

Mon colleague et moi, Brian Zatapatique, (vive Brian, le pouff célèbre) ont dit à vous au subject du Mouton Anglo-Français (avec les pommes frites). Je vous voudrai recommender ce Mouton de l'aviation, parce qu'il est le premier Mouton aéronautique dans le monde entier.

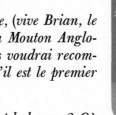

Mais, peut-être vous me demandez, où est le bagage? Où sont les voyageurs? Et maintenant – voilà! Ils sont dans l'intérior d'intestins du Mouton Anglo-Français.

Certainement, il est un bon example de l'international co-opération et particulièrement entre la France et l'Angleterre.

A toutes les fans de mon colleague (l'international pédéraste célèbre) et moi, mille francs salutations,

Brian Zatapatique et son ami

Madame Palm Writes;

Dear Madame Palm,
Our Local Building Society Branch Manager says that Insurance is illegal. Can this be true?

Ron Higgins, Cirencester.

Dear Ron, there is absolutely no need to be ashamed of your body. Sex is a perfectly natural function that all post-pubescent people indulge in. For heavens sake can't we get it out in the open?

Dear Madame Palm,
What can I do about acne? I have tried everything, creams, jellies, injections, pumice stone, dieting, tablets and mud packs, but no matter what I do my skin remains smooth and clear. Can you buy acne?
Yours hopefully,
R. Bradshaw, Biggleswade.

Dear R. Bradshaw, please believe me when I tell you that sex is absolutely normal for people of all ages and between everybody and anyone except filthy perverts who should be castrated and locked away for ever, honestly, hanging is too good for them. Love and understanding will go a long way towards curing all the ills in the world except nasty filthy perverts who should be put down at once.

Dear Madame Palm,
Can you settle a family argument? My parents say that black and white television is really in colour, but I maintain that colour TV is really black and white. Who is right?

Puzzled, Wakefield.

Dear Puzzled, sex is one of God's greatest gifts, along with nudity, golf and wrestling. Please try and understand that no matter how dirty your desires may seem they are perfectly natural.
P.S. I am sending you some leaflets. Good aren't they?

Dear Madame Palm,
I have a teensy problemette. As I was mincing down the roady-poady the other Davy daykins, I saw an absolutely divine, but divine darling-heart!, jackety-poohs in ever so soft Sammy silk. Ooh! it drove me delirious ducky-darling, but when could I wear it?

The Rev. B.J. Mitchell,
Upper Choirboy,
Gloucs.

Arson is a perfectly natural feeling, Geoffrey. How many of us at one time or another in our lives hasn't felt the need to set fire to some great public building or other. I know I have.

Dear Madame Palm,
I have a problem. You see I have bad breath. Also I am quite ugly. I am so embarrassed about this and I don't know who else to turn to for confidential advice. I am too shy to ask my family doctor and I would just die if anyone ever found out.
NAME AND ADDRESS SUPPLIED.
(Although in fact it is:
Betty Rogers,
32, The Cuttings,
Bolton.
Telephone Number:
Bolton 0123495)

Dear Betty, how many times must I keep telling you that sex is fun. I like it. You like it. Everybody likes it. Mr Robinson from the off-licence likes it twice.

Dear Sir or Madame Palm,
I, or rather a friend of mine, although I suppose I might as well be honest and say straight out that it is really me, but it may not be me, I could have a friend like it as well, but no! To be honest, it is me, suffer from indecision. Probably.
I have lost two or three or perhaps five jobs in the last day or days. Please tell me what to do. No, no, don't.
Yours faithfully or sincerely,
Stephen or Mavis Buchanan,
or Jack Noonan.

Dear All, no of course you can't get pregnant that way.

Dear Madame Palm,
Our dog Nipper has just won a seat in the U.S. Senate. Will he have to be vaccinated?
Yours, J. Wilcox, Preston.

Yes Mr Wilcox, I'm afraid all U.S. Senators have to be vaccinated.

Dear Madame Palm,
I served for eight years with the Ghurkas. We fought against incredible odds in all parts of the North Western Frontier to safeguard the freedom and the right to self-determination of the people of Southern Asia. I am now a part-time notice board in a prominent public school. I also prefer wearing women's dresses. Are there any other ex-Ghurkas similarly interested?
NAME AND RANK SUPPLIED.

Dear Name and Rank Supplied, what a lovely name. No of course you shouldn't give up. Try taking a hot bath first to relax yourself and then keep trying. Don't worry if it doesn't work at first, it'll soon become fun and practice makes perfect, as the doctors say.
There's nothing better than a jolly good

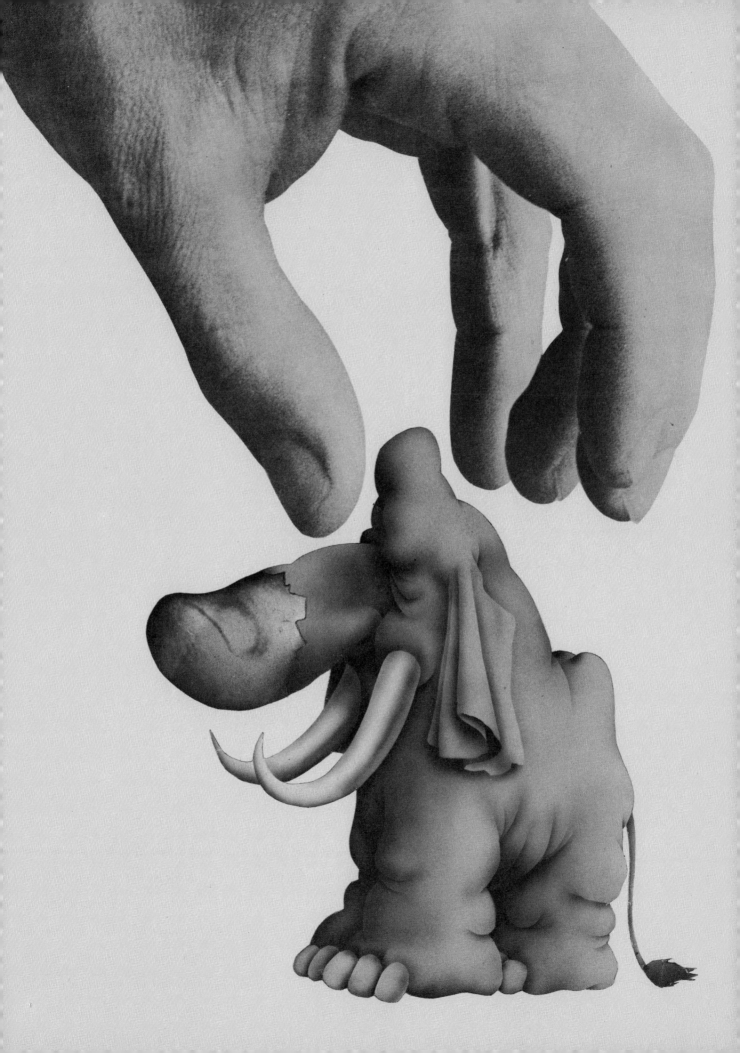

The Family Tree of Johann Gambolputty de von Ausfernschpledenschlittcrasscrenbonfriediggerdingledangle-
dongleburgsteinvonknackerthrasherapplebangerhorowitzticolensicgranderknottyspelltinklegrandlichgrumbelmeyer-
spelterwasserkurstlichhimbleeisenbahnwagengutenabendbitteeinnürnburgerbratwurstlegerspurtenmitzweimache-
luberhundsfütgumberaberschonendankerkalbsfleischmittleraucher Von Hauptkopf of Ulm.

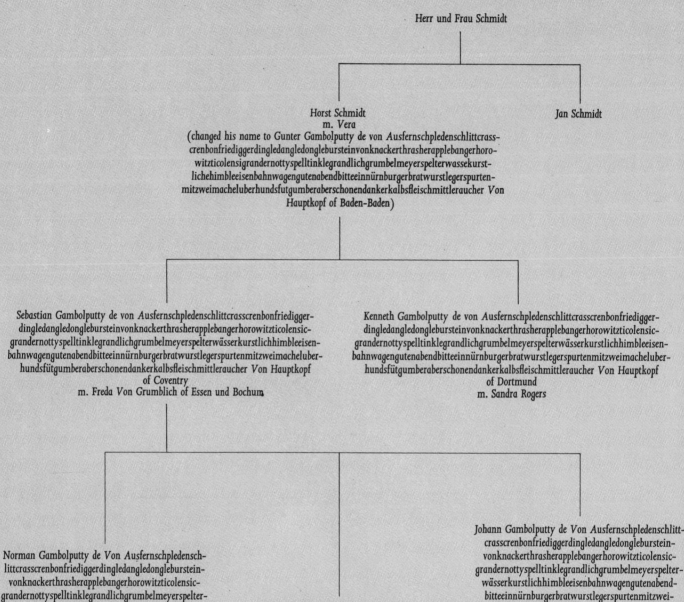

Herr und Frau Schmidt

Horst Schmidt
m. Vera
(changed his name to Gunter Gambolputty de von Ausfernschpledenschlittcrass-
crenbonfriediggerdingledangledongleburgsteinvonknackerthrasherapplebangerhoro-
witzticolensigrandernottyspelltinklegrandlichgrumbelmeyerspelterwassekurst-
lichehimbleeisenbahnwagengutenabendbitteeinnürnburgerbratwurstlegerspurten-
mitzweimacheluberhundsfutgumberaberschonendankerkalbsfleischmittleraucher Von
Hauptkopf of Baden-Baden)

Jan Schmidt

Sebastian Gambolputty de von Ausfernschpledenschlittcrasscrenbonfriedigger-
dingledangledongleburgsteinvonknackerthrasherapplebangerhorowitzticolensic-
grandernottyspelltinklegrandlichgrumbelmeyerspelterwässerkurstlichhimbleeisen-
bahnwagengutenabendbitteeinnürnburgerbratwurstlegerspurtenmitzweimacheluber-
hundsfütgumberaberschonendankerkalbsfleischmittleraucher Von Hauptkopf
of Coventry
m. Freda Von Grumblich of Essen und Bochum

Kenneth Gambolputty de von Ausfernschpledenschlittcrasscrenbonfriedigger-
dingledangledongleburgsteinvonknackerthrasherapplebangerhorowitzticolensic-
grandernottyspelltinklegrandlichgrumbelmeyerspelterwässerkurstlichhimbleeisen-
bahnwagengutenabendbitteeinnürnburgerbratwurstlegerspurtenmitzweimacheluber-
hundsfütgumberaberschonendankerkalbsfleischmittleraucher Von Hauptkopf
of Dortmund
m. Sandra Rogers

Norman Gambolputty de Von Ausfernschpledensch-
littcrasscrenbonfriediggerdingledangledongleburgstein-
vonknackerthrasherapplebangerhorowitzticolensic-
grandernottyspelltinklegrandlichgrumbelmeyerspelter-
wässerkurstlichhimbleeisenbahnwagengutenabend-
bitteeinnürnburgerbratwurstlegerspurtenmitzwei-
macheluberhundsfütgumberaberschonendankerkalbs-
fleischmittleraucher von Hauptkopf of Ulm

Karl Gambolputty de Von Ausfernschpledensch-
littcrasscrenbonfriediggerdingledangledongleburgstein-
vonknackerthrasherapplebangerhorowitzticolensic-
grandernottyspelltinklegrandlichgrumbelmeyerspelter-
wässerkurstlichhimbleeisenbahnwagengutenabend-
bitteeinnürnburgerbratwurstlegerspurtenmitzwei-
macheluberhundsfütgumberaberschonendankerkalbs-
fleischmittleraucher von Hauptkopf of Ulm

Johann Gambolputty de Von Ausfernschpledenschlitt-
crasscrenbonfriediggerdingledangledongleburgstein-
vonknackerthrasherapplebangerhorowitzticolensic-
grandernottyspelltinklegrandlichgrumbelmeyerspelter-
wässerkurstlichhimbleeisenbahnwagengutenabend-
bitteeinnürnburgerbratwurstlegerspurtenmitzwei-
macheluberhundsfütgumberaberschonendankerkalbs-
fleischmittleraucher von Hauptkopf of Ulm
m. Sarah Gambolputty de Von Ausfernschpleden-
schlittcrasscrenbonfriediggerdingledangledongleburst-
einvonknackerthrasherapplebangerhorowitzticolensic-
grandernottyspelltinklegrandlichgrumbelmeyerspelter-
wässerkurstlichhimbleeisenbahnwagengutenabend-
bitteeinnürnburgerbratwurstlegerspurtenmitzwei-
macheluberhundsfütgumberaberschonendankerkalbs-
fleischmittleraucher Von Hauptkopf of Ulm nee —
Sarah Grumblebittekunsthausunderdemlindenwir-
makenmanknochtlichmitkartofelnundknopfelsindem-
tischhabtmandiekucherbittejahwoldingleneinschtill-
enachtheilgenachtallesschlaftalleswelsichbinein-
Berlinermanundwoistderherrenbittevielenddnkerapples-
chtrudeleidelweissmachelubehundsfutmitteinegrosse-
bierebitte Von Hauptkopf of München.

RADIO TIMES marks the world's premier race with a 4-page special feature.

The Greatest Upper Class Race in the World

Grandstand: Saturday 3.20 BBC1 Colour.
Sportsnight with Bakewell: Monday 10.00 am. BBC2. Sepia.

The Race

"Her Majesty the Queen has always wanted win this Race and certainly this year she nds an excellent chance."

Immortal

1836 Captain Oliver Piccarda-Messel bet Colonel Sammy Beecher that his son was greater twit than any alive that day. stantly they repaired to some adjoining lds and shot each other dead. An every-y story perhaps, but from just this wager ew the now world famous race which is alled only by the Irish Religious Classic d The Rich Sons of Boston III ce. Yet neither of these two have the peal of The Twits. Maybe its just that English Upper Classes do specialise breeding such a fine strain of thorough-d twit.

Curry

Certainly the English Public Schools play a strong part in encouraging the right sort of chap to exterminate himself publicly on the playing fields of the world. Rugby Union must take much of the praise for this. From an early age small upper class boys are encouraged to run headlong into large groups of heavier boys in a vain attempt to avoid brain damage. From this is developed a spirit of fair play and a ruthless refusal to question any order – no matter how idiotic. This sensibility is further encouraged by a short stay in the Guards, where the apprentice twit is shown how to fall off horses, how to fall on parade in front of Her Majesty, and how to fall over drunk in Kensington disco-thèques. The final accolade comes when he is permitted to join the MCC. Now he *is* fully prepared for the Race.

Biscuit Barrel

It is rightly described as a handicap – most of the entrants have more than one – and in practice almost anyone can win providing they have remembered to enter. To the winner it's worth far more than the traditional five thousand guineas and a decent military burial; the perks are enormous. He can, if he so specifies before the race, be carried around the world's American Air Bases with Bob Hope, and he will certainly get his photograph in Jennifer's Diary (*the* accolade for most aristocracy); but above all he will be allowed to bear for twelve months the coveted title of Upper Class Twit of the Year.

Norman St. John Thing takes the matchbox jump, 1970. Norman's hobby was falling over. He fell over for Britain in the 1968 Olympics.

Victory for Lt. Colonel Morris's son Justin in 1971. He runs himself over magnificently, and into first place at the 6th.

iver Seaton-Mollusc comes in first as the 1971 pper Class Twit.

The Course

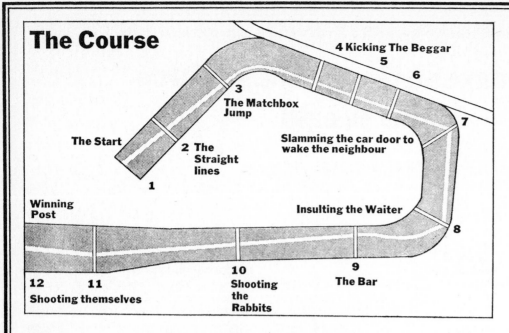

The Start

1

2 The Straight lines

3 The Matchbox Jump

4 Kicking The Beggar

5

6

7

Slamming the car door to wake the neighbour

Insulting the Waiter

8

Winning Post

12   **11**

Shooting themselves

10 Shooting the Rabbits

9 The Bar

The race itself

David Coleman, In conversation with A. Writer.

1 The Start
A difficult one is this. Many of the Twits fail to get off to any kind of start whatsoever. In 1967 a Captain Brough-Oyster was a faller on his way into the stadium, and tragically had to be put down.

2 The Straight Lines
The great thing is not to take these too fast. They can be coped with more easily if the Twit imagines they are Harrods corridors.

3 The Matchbox Jump
A good Twit will take this accidentally.

4 Kicking the Beggar
The field is beginning to stagger a lot h so you can take your time. The Judge disqualify you if you kick the Beggar a he's down more than eight times. Ma great twits have gone out at this simply through kicking the Judge. In 1 O. K. S. J. St. P. Semaphore went ou racing altogether when he accident. kicked three Irish Clergy and they about him.

5 Hunt Ball Photograph
The Twit must face the Camera. He m also try and remember to kiss the Deb not one of the other Twits.
Now come three easier obstacles; first

6 Reversing into the Old Lady
An easy one this for the average T' Also he is for once off his own w enemy – his feet – and into an expens automobile. Oliver was a spectacular fa here in '71, bringing himself down fr behind. Incidentally, a firm in Surbi supplies the old ladies.

7 Slamming the Car Door to wake the Neighbour
Second nature to Kensington dwell County entrants might have a little d culty here.

8 Insulting the Waiter
Again second nature, especially if waiter's from a proper working-class ho and not just a foreigner.

Some famous Twits

Nigel Incubator-Jones, leading the field at the sixth. Accidentally managed to survive the race in 1970 and is now trained and run professionally in America.

Nigel Nigel Hyphen Hyphen Stroke Money. Winner 1961. A really excellent Twit. Beat a boy to death at Eton for being middle class.

Gervaise Brooke-Hamster. Was a part-time paper basket for his father whilst he was tr for the race which he won in 1963 when all the entrants sank.

The Bar

rhaps the most difficult after the Debs. ey must walk under the bar without ining themselves. Most take 5 or 6 goes. e winning post is in sight now as they ne to the tenth.

) Shooting the Rabbits

ey are of course tied down but this in t makes it more difficult as it removes chance of the animals accidentally unding themselves. They can hear the wd again now as they race for the nous eleventh.

1 Taking the Bra off the Debs

mmies are used nowadays as occasion- y the Debs got excited. It's a good idea let your twits see a bra before the race. ost have little knowledge of its existence, function or its fastening. ally into the Grandstand finish and the rious twelfth –

2 Shooting themselves

is requires less skill than might be agined, for Brigadier Henry Butcher in History of the Race claims that nearly y per cent of all Twits are shot accident- y by the others. Still, they all count on e scorecard, and whilst the actual win- r is probably stiffening somewhere back the Course, there's many a second and rd been picked up here at the final ole.

only remains for the Visiting Royalty to corate the Winner's coffin with the ele- nt Medals (designed by Lord Snowden m an idea by David Hockney) and then s on to Kensington for the traditional ti Spumante and car-door slamming.

ous stud this – Major Sebastian Brake-Smythe . Accidentally reproduced himself at the Deb Year Show, Olympia, when he fell down some His son is studying Income Tax at Cambridge.

1. Justin is a faller at the 3rd.

2. Oliver brilliantly puts the boot in on the beggar at the 4th.

3. Nigel Incubator-Jones gleefully leads the field at The Bra.

4. The Notorious Bar.

5. The Rabbits.

1

2

3

4

5

What to look for in a Great Twit

Head. Look for thickness. This is what makes for outstanding Twitting. Military training is an obvious advantage here.

The Face. Look for absence of expression. Is he really vacant? If he is, make for the Tote.

Tie. An important clue to breeding. MCC ties are the favourite, closely followed by Eton, Harrow and the Guards.

Watch. Probably ludicrously expens Probably stopped.

The naughty bits. Are they completely dormant? Most of them are after leaving Public School but occasionally disasters occur. Simon Main Waring Waring Main had to be pulled off one of the dummies in 1969.

Feet. The best twits try to keep as few on the ground as possible. Rugby helps.

Balance. A good Twit should have none whatsoever.

Next Week in the Radio Times

Derek Nimmo will be starting a n series and finishing some old ones. Mari Goring discusses comedy with Rita Wel and A. J. P. Taylor. Rod McKuen will looking at some pussy cats. Paul Fox d cusses *The Six Repeats of Henry VI* BBC 2
Film: *The Making of Philip Jenkinso* Viewers will be shown round whilst Phi Jenkinson is actually put together.

Full list of Runners on Page 13. That's between Pages 12 and 9 of your new-style Radio Times.

LUMBERJACK SONG

Chorus by the men of the Royal Canadian Mounted Police.

1. I'm a lumberjack
    And I'm O.K.
    I sleep all night
    And I work all day.

    He's a lumberjack
    And he's O.K.
    He sleeps all night
    And he works all day.

2. I cut down trees
    I eat my lunch
    I go to the lavatory
    On Wednesday I go shopping
    And have buttered scones for tea.

    Mounties He cuts down trees
    He eats his lunch
    He goes to the lavatory
    On Wednesday he goes shopping
    And has buttered scones for tea.

    He's a lumberjack
    And he's O.K.
    He sleeps at night
    And he works all day.

3. I cut down trees
    I skip and jump
    I like to press wild flowers
    I put on women's clothing
    And hang around in bars.

    Mounties He cuts down trees
    He skips and jumps
    He likes to press wild flowers
    He puts on women's clothing
    And hangs around in bars.

    He's a lumberjack
    And he's O.K.
    He sleeps all night
    And he works all day.

4. I cut down trees
    I wear high heels
    Suspenders and a bra
    I wish I'd been a girlie
    Just like my dear Pappa.

    Mounties He cuts down trees
    He wears high heels
    (spoken rather than sung)
    Suspenders . . . and a bra ?
    That's shocking, etc.
    That's rude . . . tuttut . . . tut
    tut . . .
    (music runs down)

Do-it-yourself Story

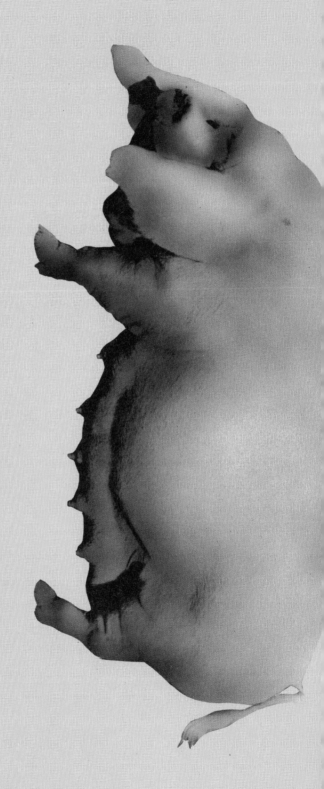

It was a dark, stormy   The wind
through the trees. A creak was heard on the stair. A howl in the
dark was heard and there, crouching in the black arch of the old
manse was the most hideously   creature I had ever
seen. It was shaped like a   , over its head it wore a   ,
and its one eye   from its   and rolled
down its scaly chest. Seeing it was about to   on me, I
leaped into the shadows and pulled out my   The Creature
took one look and let out a great   with pink
ribbons. But I ignored it, and rushed headlong at it, twirling my
          above my   with   under its   at the
back of the   without any

It was several days later that I returned to the scene of this
terrifying encounter, and discovered to my infinite horror
                    under a bush. I was so surprised to
see the Prime Minister   with a bit of burnt
cork, that I could not help but let out a   immedi-
ately told me not to be so old-fashioned and showed me a
which I had never seen before, except in   s.

But surely, Gerald," I exclaimed, "You can't
with one of those!"

Gerald grinned and   up in a tree. Whereupon
the Prime   threw his   over his back
and   his   into a large bowl on the grass. Amazement
spread across my face, as I saw the Leader of the House of
Commons   a small piece of   and eat it,
pausing only to   his   into another
large bowl. Meanwhile, the Leader of the Opposition suddenly
appeared from behind Mrs   who was not in the best
of moods, having just   Roy Jenkins with a
          without letting it dry. The Speaker then produced
a bucket and proceeded to   the   left by
the   in his hat.

"What on Earth is going on?" I cried.

To be continued   week.

Words you might find useful

Marsupial, Derry & Toms, turbot, trenchant, bird, fish, restaurant, albumen, fin, last, protruding, nasty lumps, mackerel, hake,
lamprey, temper, surprise, mackintosh, Harringay Stadium,
reputable, desuetude, lobster mayonnaise, herring gull, Great
Barrier Reef, witness, defy, pike, Reginald, "VOM-IT" PRO-
DUCTS LTD., smashed, avuncular, nape, Grimsby, Lowestoft,
trawler, fleet, net, catch, trawl, gill, tail-fin, fillets, slab, Shirley,
smoked, white sauce, with chips, deep-fried, jellied, potted,
fingers, for supper, lunch, or, tea, yum-yum, mmmmmm, ah,
fishy, fishy, fish.

Goats' Page

Yes! Another British publishing first! A page entirely for goats . . . It contains: news, views, quizzes and features aimed specifically at horned ruminants.

Hello, goats! First a quiz:

Quiz

1. How many goats have stood for Parliament?
   - a) 1
   - b) 70
   - c) none

2. What animal can swallow a sheep whole?
   - a) a goat
   - b) an anaconda

3. Who was the famous Notts and England fast bowler who figured in the body-line controversy of the early 1930s?
   - a) Harold Larwood
   - b) a goat

4. Which goat wrote 'Oliver Twist'?
   - a) Smokey   b) Billy Boy
   - c) Jacko   d) Tin-Tin
   - e) Not a goat at all

Answers

1. none
2. an anaconda
3. Harold Larwood
4. Not a goat at all

Quotes about goats

What Famous People Have Said About Goats:

   - a) Milton: nothing
   - b) Robespierre: nothing
   - c) Dante: nothing
   - d) William Pitt the Elder: "I must go and put a goat on" (poss. misheard – Ed.)
   - e) Henry Ford: nothing
   - f) Clodagh Rodgers: nothing
   - g) Keith Miller (Great Australian all-rounder of the 1950s): nothing

Where to eat in London for Goats

   - a) Hyde Park
   - b) Regents Park
   - c) Hampstead Heath
   - d) The Quality Restaurant, Tottenham Street

Advice to Goats

1. Progressive tail-mange is best treated by eating the grass around Elm trees.

2. Loss of beard-hair in nanny-goats is best treated by The Trichological Clinic, Mayfair (appointments only).

3. It has come to our notice that boa-constrictors have been passing themselves off as goats in order to get into cheese commercials. Check your contracts! Ring: Goats' Equity.

4. The long-awaited second volume of Prof. Hockstetter's absorbing study of *Medieval Church Life in Tuscany Dei Fiorenze Angelici* is to be published next January by Eyre & Spottiswoode, price 6gns. It is best eaten uncooked or torn into little pieces with some nettles.

5. All goats should avoid: "The Holiday Homes For Pets Pie Co. Ltd".

6. Goats with speech defects are reminded that they can get up to 50% discount on photographic equipment.

A message from Tonto

Once again it's been a bad year for goats, with humans confirming their ascendency in the vital fields of politics, economics, education and technological achievements. Only in the Arts and in the mountains have goats maintained their supremacy. Eton, Harrow and many other top public schools are still closed to goats, and, of the Services, only the R.A.F. allows goats to take up anything other than short-service commissions. Fashion still passes us by, and when did you last see a goat on Top Of The Pops?

If we are to change this at all, we must learn to THINK GOAT. Don't think of yourself as the plaything of Alpine milkmaids, the mascot of the Irish Guards . . . Think of yourself as a GOAT. Don't be compromised by the R.S.P.C.A. . . . remember GOAT IS GREAT! Right On!

yours

Tonto

P.S. Do not eat this message

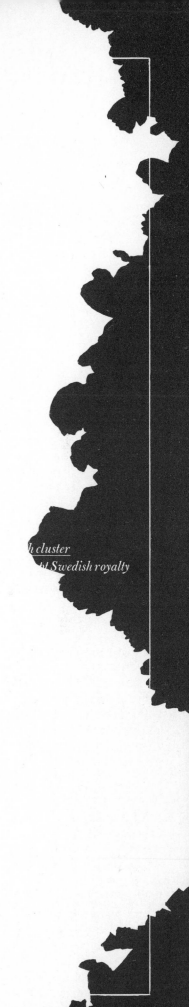

h cluster
t Swedish royalty

HELLO O.N.s EVERYWHERE

Last year's Founders Day Service in the School Chapel was well attended.

As usual news of the old boys has been flowing in from the branches. **Ribbentrop, Von** (NAZIS 1930-45) is working as a night-club hostess in Bristol. He says he's really happy meeting new people and doesn't miss being foreign minister at all. However he's managed to work some of his diplomatic experience into his night-club act, when he performs the Treaty of Brest-Litovsk dance, in which he manages to combine the salient features of Russo-German relations in the later half of the 1930's with the music of Burt Bacharach. Keep it up Ron!

Good news also from **Hilter, A.** (NAZIS 1923-45). He has just landed a very good job with a Steel Band, after some difficult times as a roadie (*A Road Manager's Assistant in a Pop Group –Ed.*). He plays at University Balls and is also in great demand for masonics, charity functions but not Bar Mitzvahs where his act is considered offensive! And remembering Adolf and the tuckshop owner we can imagine why!! He has great plans for the band, including the annexation of Poland and the creation of Lebensraum in the Balkans.

Not such good news from **Bormann, M.** (NAZIS 1931-45). His non-Nazi boutique in Guatemala City went bankrupt last May, when a nuclear weapon was discovered in one of the changing-rooms. Martin is now working in New York, and has changed his name to Goldberg.

Bimmler, H. (NAZIS 1923-45) is in Rep. in the Argentine. Recently he played opposite another old boy **McGoering, H.** (NAZIS 1923-45) in 'The Reluctant Debutante'. The critics gave unanimous praise to the production. The Pampas Herald wrote "Hermann McGoering as the dotty mother-in-law was a most interesting piece of characterisation. Strutting about the stage in a field-grey uniform, banging his fists and haranguing the audience over loadspeakers, he brought a vividness and excitement to an otherwise rather dull role, and in the scene with Beryl outside Boodle's Club, the speech about the expansion of the Luftwaffe was a most interesting addition to the text."

Our next O.N.s get-together will, we hope, be organised in Johannesburg by

J. Goebbels-Smythe (NAZIS 1923-4 who is in Public Relations the There'll be a chance to see some of t old Leni Riefenstahl films and the will be a Son et Lumière re-enactme of Dunkirk in aid of the Reichst rebuilding fund. We hope as ma O.N.s as possible will turn out, b do remember to have plastic surge first. Remember what happened **Eichmann, A.** (NAZIS 1932-45).

Goodbye for now, O.N.s ever where. Our next newsletter will available in January and we are hopi it will be the largest, fastest, mc powerful newsletter in the worl Capable of complete Mobilisation 24 hours! Ready to deliver a death blc at the enemy's oilfields, before he ca get off the ground! It will be printed special paper to last a thousand yea ORDER YOUR COPY NOW!

The rebuilding of the Reichstag, New Pavilion and Quiet Room are now well advanced.

Whizzo Assortment

Crunchy frog
tiniest baby frog, dew picked and flown from Iraq, cleansed in finest quality spring water, lightly killed and sealed in a succulent Swiss quintuple-smooth full-cream treble milk chocolate envelope, and lovingly frosted with glucose.

Cherry fondue
extremely nasty

Cockroach cluster
enjoyed by royalty, except Swedish royalty

Anthrax ripple
America's favourite

Ram's bladder cup
only the choicest juicy chunks of fresh Cornish Ram's bladder, emptied, steamed, flavoured with sesame seeds, whipped into a fondue and garnished with lark's vomit

Spring surprise
our speciality! dark smooth chocolate. When you pop it in your mouth steel bolts spring out and plunge straight through both cheeks

as recommended by Superintendant Parrot of the Hygene Squad
Contains plenty of monosodium glutomate and lark's vomit

English	Hungarian
At the tobacconists:	*In the abbatoir:*
How much is that?	You have beautiful thighs.
Have you change for a pound?	My hovercraft is full of eels.
I want twenty cigarettes please.	If I said you had a beautiful bod would you hold it against me?
Oh, and some matches.	I am no longer infected.
Do you want them plain or filter tipped?	Do you want to come back to place bouncy bouncy?
I would also like some sweets.	Drop your panties, Sir Willia I cannot wait until lunchtime.
Thank you very much.	Great boobies, honeybunch.
Can you direct me to the railway station?	Please fondle my bum.

How to walk silly

ohnson's Novelties

aranteed amusing As used by the crowned heads of Europe. Has brought
rs to the eyes of Royalty. "Denmark has never laughed so much."
e Stage.

A "Naughty Humphrey"
Breaks the ice at parties. Put it on the table.
Press the button. It vomits. Absolutely
authentic. Fully guaranteed. With refills.

ck Soap

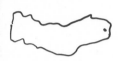

ave it in the bathroom. They wash their
nds: real fungus grows on the fingers.
solutely guaranteed. Breaks the ice at
ties.

For drinks why not buy a Wicked Willy
With a life-sized winkle. Serves warm beer.
Makes cocktails. Hours of amusement.

ghten the elderly
al snakes. Just watch them run.

Hours of fun with "Honeymoon Delight"
Empty it into their beds. Real skunk juice.
They won't forget their wedding night.
Sticks to the skin. Absolutely waterproof.
Guaranteed to break the ice at parties.

aughty nightie

it on. It melts. Breaks the ice at naughty
ties.

Comedy Hernia Kit
Plastic flesh wounds. Keep your friend in
stitches. Breaks the ice at parties.

h Pooh machine

barrass your guests. Completely
hentic sound. Breaks the ice at parties.

JOURNEY INTO EARL'S COURT

A Raw Tale Of Bed-sitter Land by the Author of: *"Percy F. Westerman"*.

Once upn. tme. there lvd. 2 grls 1 gent. shrd. rm Earls Ct. One dy. Jack mt 3rd grl with bg. bsms. he cld. hdly blve his eyes. "My gd." he thght. "I bt. sh bngs lke sht-hse. dr". Jack st nxt. to grl & sd: "Whr. do you cme frm, Brstl?" The grl knckd. hm rnd. hd. wth her hndbg. "Yah sckr! Pss ff" she sd. Jck ws unccstmd. hring grls tlk. lke tht., so he ht. hr strght. btwn. th eyes, & wnt hme to hs 2 grls. & lvd hpply evr. aftr.

Moral: When there are two courses of action open to a man, that which leads to forgiveness, when the choice is clear, is not necessarily the choice which will, in the final analysis, provide a basis for a settlement on the issues discussed in the Berlin Conference 1964.

Second Moral: Many a moral makes fair reading.

Third Moral: It is a wise moral that knows when to stop.

Fourth Moral: A wise moral is hard to find but a chicken lays an egg only once.

Our Agricultural Correspondent writes: "This is not strictly true. Many chickens lay two or three eggs in one day".
(Our Agricultural Correspondent has not quite got the point of the moral – Ed.)

ANIMAL LOVERS' COLUMN

A Message For All Animal Lovers: Your practice is illegal and punishable by a heavy fine and up to seven years imprisonment.

---

e Showbiz Bit
with a Foreword by Helen Shapiro*

1. The anagram game

The following are anagrams of famous showbiz stars:
a. Des O'Connro
b. Dadiv Frost
c. Cilla Balck
d. Eamonn Andrews

Answers:
1. Des O'Connor
2. David Frost
3. Cilla Black
4. Nora W. Deensman
Max. points: 4

2. Who are they now?

Which stars had these names before they became popular:
a. Des O'Boils
b. David Titty
c. Frank Black
d. Eamonn Andrews

Answers:
a. David Frost
b. Cilla Black
c. David Frost
d. Nora W. Deensman
Max. points: 4   Min. points: 18

3. Showbiz riddle-me-ree

My first is in Kirk Douglas
But not in Monica Vitti
My second is in Rock Hudson
But not in Britt Ekland
My third is in Burt Lancaster
But not in Julie Christie
My fourth is in Dirk Bogarde
But not in Pet Clark
My whole is in Troy Donahue
What am I?

Answer: An old poove
Max. points: 1

Total: 15 points or over: Very good.
10 or over: Excellent.
Less than 10: Not bad.
5 or under: Very good.

*sorry, this is not true

4

5

6

Be A Modern Hermit

Get Away From It All

In pleasant modern surroundings in a smart newly-erected Hermit Estate near Bradford.

Live in comfortable solitude with nice neighbours within easy walking distance of shopping precinct. Still some semi-detached caves (use of W/C. k. & b.) to let, rent or buy near Pringles Wood (Nearest Tube Nth. Hampstead).

Meditate in private at the Sunshine Hermitage Hilton. Suites fully bookable. Parties catered for.

Get your Hermitcard

Can be exchanged for nuts, mud, berries, bits of string, wattle or rush at any branch of Barclays, Lloyds or Coutts with a Hermit-check.

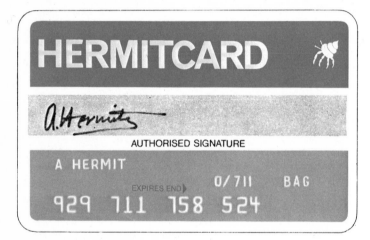

Invest in Real Estate

Enjoy an assured income as a hermit.

Join the Hermit Real Estate Assured Financial Mortgage Protection International Investors Group.

Hermitours

Get away from them all with our smart range of modern tours
16 weeks in the Gobi Desert.
3 week winter chastisement holiday in Zurich.
Trans-Atlantic Los Angeles Pray-In. (Concession via Cha hermits Ltd)
Flagellation fortnight at the Berlin Beer Festival.
Or go to Hermins: Clacton, Bognor, Pwllheli. A friendly a phere, child-minding service, sport, entertainment. Chalets e

Or Win

A weekend for two with a Rod, Pole or Perch.
A life subscription to HERMIT/QUEEN.
A visit to Royal Ascot.

Just put the reasons in the correct order. I wanted to beco hermit because of the
mortgage
new pubs
whist drives
launderette service.

For YOU at Age 65

A holiday cave of your own in Torremolinos.
1000 nuts in cash.
Your own penthouse cave wattled in a colour of your own ch

Previous Famous Hermits

Billy Wright.
Chuter Ede.
S. Baldwin.

Personal

3rd Hermit required to share basement cave – Dulwich. Must own nuts. Box 14.
Hermits get discounts at Gorringes on all G-Plan furniture.
4th Butch Chartered Accountant wanted for parties. Will swa

he Poems of Ewen McTeagle

Lines Written to Lassie O'Shea

> '*To Ma Own Beloved Mary.*
> *A poem on her 17th birthday.*'

> *Lend us a couple of bob till Thursday,*
> *I'm absolutely skint*
> *But I'm expecting a postal order*
> *And I can pay you back*
> *As soon as it comes.*

The recurrence of this theme of desperate search, for something perhaps symbolic, perhaps half imagined, is central to his greatest work: 'Can I have £50 to mend the shed.'

> *Can I have Fifty pounds to mend the shed?*
> *I'm right on my Uppers.*
> *I can pay you back*
> *When I get this postal order from Australia*
> *Honestly.*
> *Hope the bladder trouble's getting better.*
> *Love, Ewen?*

Other Poems: 'My new cheque book hasn't arrived', 'Lend us a bob for a wee refreshment, hen', 'What's twenty quid to the bloody Midland Bank?', 'I'll just have to cut down on food'.

Prize Winning Poem to the Arts Council: 'Can you lend me a £1000 quid?' (This poem won £1)

e Poems of Ewen McTeagle
oduced by the Lionel Blair Dancers*

m the lonely crofts of Scotland, two three turn, from the nts of coot and hern, pause kick, comes a still small voice in orld gone mad, jump two three down, round, spin: the try of Ewen McTeagle. This young Scottish poet, up two e, spin, jump and down, has taken the world of literature by throat, pause, kick kick pause, with such poems as 'Spare 50p for a cup of tea, Guv' and the world famous 'Lend us a d till the end of the week'.

> *Lend us a quid till the end of the week.*
> *If you could see your way*
> *To lending me sixpence*
> *I could at least buy a newspaper.*
> *That's not much to ask anyone.*

on Reading Chapman's *Homer* in Selfridges

> *Owe gie to me a shillin for some fags*
> *And I'll pay yer back on Thursday.*
> *But if you can wait till Saturday*
> *I'm expecting a divvy from the*
> *Harpenden Building Society.*

*The Lionel Blair Dancers would like to thank Dr John A. G. 'Honest to God' Robinson for his help on the choreography.

THE PIRANHA BROTHERS

Last Tuesday a reign of terror was ended when the notorious Piranha brothers, Doug and Dinsdale, after one of the most extraordinary trials in British legal history, were sentenced to 400 years imprisonment for crimes of violence. We examined the rise to power of the Piranhas, the methods they used to subjugate rival gangs and their subsequent tracking down and capture by the brilliant Superintendent Harry 'Snapper' Organs of Q Division.

Doug and Dinsdale Piranha were born, on probation, in a small house in Kipling Road, Southwark, the eldest sons in a family of sixteen. Their father

Arthur Piranha, the father of Doug and Dinsdale

Arthur Piranha, a scrap metal dealer and TV quizmaster, was well known to the police, and a devout Catholic. In January 1928 he had married Kitty Malone, an up-and-coming East End boxer. Doug was born in February 1929 and Dinsdale two weeks later; and again a week after that. Someone who remembers them well was their next door neighbour, Mrs April Simnel.

"Oh yes Kipling Road was a typical East End Street, people were in and out of each other's houses with each others' property all day. They were a cheery lot. Cheerful and violent. Doug was keen on boxing, but when he learned to walk he took up putting the boot in the groin. He was very interested in that. His mother had a terrible job getting him to come in for his tea. Putting his little boot in he'd be, bless him. All the kids were like that then, they didn't have their heads stuffed with all this Cartesian dualism."

At the age of fifteen Doug and Dinsdale started attending the Ernest Pythagoras Primary School in Clerkenwell. When the Piranhas left school they were called up but were found by an Army Board to be too mentally unstable even for National Service. Denied the opportunity to use their talents in the service of their country, they began to operate what they called 'The Operation' . . . They would select a victim and then threaten to beat him up if he paid them the so-called protection money. Four months later they started another operation which they called 'The Other Operation'. In this racket they selected another victim and threatened not to beat him up if he didn't pay them. One month later they hit upon 'The Other Other Operation'. In this the victim was threatened that if he didn't pay them, they would beat him up. This for the Piranha brothers was the turning point.

Doug and Dinsdale Piranha now formed a gang which they called 'The Gang' and used terror to take over night clubs, billiard halls, gaming casinos and race tracks. When they tried to take over the MCC they were for the only time in their lives, slit up a treat. As their empire spread however, Q Division, were keeping tabs on their every movement by reading the colour supplements.

One small-time operator who fell foul of Dinsdale Piranha was Vince Snetterton-Lewis.

"Well one day I was at home threatening the kids when I looks out through the hole in the wall and sees this tank pull up and out gets one of Dinsdale's boys, so he come in nice and friendly and says Dinsdale wants to have a word with me, so he chains me to the back of the tank and takes me for a scrape round to Dinsdale's place and

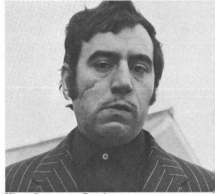

Vince Snetterton Lewis

Dinsdale's there in the conversation with Doug and Charles Paisley, the ba[...] crusher, and two film producers and a m[...] they called 'Kierkegaard', who just s[...] there biting the heads off whippets a[...] Dinsdale just says 'I hear you've been [...] naughty boy Clement' and he splits [...] nostrils open and saws me leg off and pu[...] me liver out and I tell him me name's n[...] Clement and then . . . he loses his temp[...] and nails me head to the floor."

Superintendent Harry 'Snapper' Organs Q division

continu[...]

Doug and Dinsdale
Do come!
LBJ.

The Inaugural Committee
requests the honor of your presence
and participate in the Inauguration of

Lyndon Baines Johnson
President of the United States of America
and

Hubert Horatio Humphrey
as Vice President of the United States of America
on Wednesday the twentieth of January
one thousand nine hundred and sixty-five
in the City of Washington

Kodak
READY-MOUNT

A well known
criminologist

1. Doug and Dinsdale Piranha.
2. In their heyday the Piranhas were invited
   to all kinds of social functions.
3. The gang.   4. Kitty Malone.

attractive to women.

Another man who had his head nailed to the floor was Stig O'Tracy.

Stig O'Tracy

ROGERS: "I've been told Dinsdale Piranha nailed your head to the floor."

STIG: "No. Never. He was a smashing bloke. He used to buy his mother flowers and that. He was like a brother to me."

ROGERS: "But the police have film of Dinsdale actually nailing your head to the floor."

STIG: "Oh yeah, he did that."

ROGERS: "Why?"

STIG: "Well he had to, didn't he? I mean there was nothing else he could do, be fair. I had transgressed the unwritten law."

ROGERS: "What had you done?"

STIG: "Er . . . well he didn't tell me that, but he gave me his word that it was the case, and that's good enough for me with old Dinsy. I mean, he didn't *want* to nail my head to the floor. I had to insist. He wanted to let me off. He'd do anything for you, Dinsdale would."

ROGERS: "And you don't bear him a grudge?"

STIG: "A grudge! Old Dinsy. He was a real darling."

ROGERS: "I understand he also nailed your wife's head to a coffee table. Isn't that true Mrs O'Tracy?"

MRS O'TRACY: "No, no, no, no, no, no, no, no, no, no."

STIG: "Well he did do that, yeah. He was a hard man. Vicious but fair."

Vince Snetterton-Lewis agreed with this judgement.

"Yes, definitely he was fair. After he nailed me head to the table, I used to go round every Sunday lunchtime to his flat and apologise, and then we'd shake hands and he'd nail me head to the floor. He was very reasonable. Once, one Sunday I told him my parents were coming round to tea and would he mind very much not nailing my head that week and he agreed and just screwed my pelvis to a cake stand."

Clearly Dinsdale inspired tremendous fear among his business associates. But what was he really like?

Gloria Pules knew him intimately.

"I walked out with Dinsdale on many occasions, and found him a charming and erudite companion. He was wont to introduce one to eminent celebrities, celebrated American singers, members of the aristocracy and other gang leaders, who he had met through his work for charities. He took a warm interest in Boys' Clubs, Sailors' Homes, Choristers' Associations and the Grenadier Guards."

Gloria Pules

"Mind you there was nothing unusual about him. I should say not. Except, that Dinsdale was convinced that he was being watched by a giant hedgehog whom he referred to as 'Spiny Norman'. Normally Spiny Norman was wont to be about twelve feet from snout to tail, but when Dinsdale was depressed Norman could be anything up to eight hundred yards long. When Norman was about Dinsdale would go very quiet and start wobbling and his nose would swell up and his teeth would move about and he'd get very violent and claim that he'd laid Stanley Baldwin."

ROGERS: "Did it worry you that he, for example, stitched people's legs together?"

GLORIA: "Well it's better than bottling it up isn't it. He was a gentleman, Dinsdale, and what's more he knew how to treat a female impersonator."

But what do the criminologists think? We asked The Amazing Kargol and Janet:

"It is easy for us to judge Dinsdale Piranha too harshly. After all he only did

Norman Bricks had his head nailed to a 16 weight by the Piranha Brothers when he fo their birthday.

what many of us simply dream of doing. I'm sorry. After all we should remem that a murderer is only an extrover suicide. Dinsdale was a looney, but he w happy looney. Lucky bugger."

Most of the strange tales conc Dinsdale but what of Doug? One man v met him was Luigi Vercotti.

"I had been running a successful es agency – high class, no really, high c girls . . . we didn't have any of *that* – t was right out. So I decided to open a h class night club for the gentry at Bigg wade with International cuisine and cook and top line acts, and not a cheap clip j for picking up tarts . . . that was right ou deny that completely, and one evening walks Dinsdale with a couple of big lads, of whom was carrying a tactical nucl missile. They said I had bought one of t fruit machines and would I pay for it? T wanted three quarters of a million poun I thought about it and I decided not to g the Police as I had noticed that the lad v

Luigi Vercotti

thermonuclear device was the chief
stable for the area. So a week later they
ed again and told me the cheque had
nced and said . . . I had to see . . . Doug.
Well, I was terrified. Everyone was
ified of Doug. I've seen grown men pull
r own heads off rather than see Doug.
n Dinsdale was frightened of Doug. He
d . . . sarcasm. He knew all the tricks,
natic irony, metaphor, bathos, puns,
dy, litotes and . . . satire. He was
us."

n this way, by a combination of violence
sarcasm the Piranha brothers by Feb-
y 1966 controlled London and the
th East of England. It was in February,
ugh, that Dinsdale made a big mistake.
atterly Dinsdale had become increas-
y worried about Spiny Norman. He had
e to the conclusion that Norman slept
n aeroplane hangar at Luton Airport.
l so on Feb 22nd 1966, Dinsdale blew up
on.

Even the police began to sit up and take
notice. The Piranhas realised they had
gone too far and that the hunt was on. They
went into hiding. But it was too late. Harry
'Snapper' Organs was on their trail.

"I decided on a subtle approach, viz.
some form of disguise, as the old helmet and
boots are a bit of a giveaway. Luckily my
years with Bristol Rep. stood me in good
stead, as I assumed a bewildering variety of
disguises. I tracked them to Cardiff, posing
as the Reverend Smiler Egret. Hearing
they'd gone back to London I assumed the
identity of a pork butcher, Brian Stoats. On
my arrival in London I discovered they had
returned to Cardiff, I followed as Gloucester
from *King Lear*. Acting on a hunch I spent
several months in Buenos Aires as Blind
Pew returning through the Panama Canal
as Ratty, in *Toad of Toad Hall*. Back in
Cardiff, I relived my triumph as Sancho
Panza in *Man of la Mancha* which the

Bristol Evening Post described as 'a glitter-
ing performance of rare perception', although the *Bath Chronicle* was less than
enthusiastic. In fact it gave me a right
panning. I quote 'as for the performance of
Superintendent Harry "Snapper" Organs
as Sancho Panza, the audience were be-
mused by his high-pitched Welsh accent
and intimidated by his abusive ad-libs.' The
Western Daily News said 'Sancho Panza
(Mr Organs) spoilt an otherwise impeccably
choreographed rape scene by his un-
scheduled appearance and persistent cries
of 'What's all this then ?' "

Against this kind of opposition for the
Piranha Brothers the end was inevitable. ❧

THE END

Spiny Norman

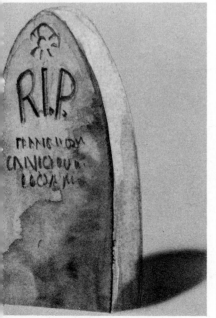

'*Other other other operation*'

avestone

The Honourable Mr Justice Retired

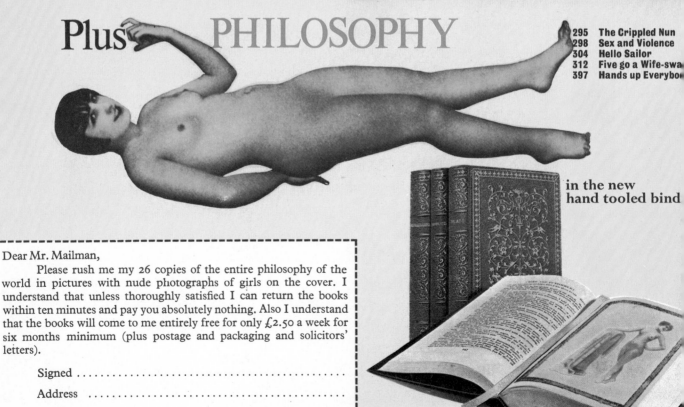

Independent Television News Limited   **ITN House 48 Wells Street London W1P 3FE**

Phone: 01-637 2424
Telex: 22101
Cables: Telindep London PS4

Pythons
Monty Python's Big Red Book

Friday

Dear Pythons

Because of all the bitterness and recriminations surrounding my Foreword I
should like to retract my endorsement of your book. It was never my
intention to arouse the antagonism of my rivals and colleagues, upon whose
wholehearted respect and co-operation I depend.

In any case, Methuen have commissioned a News at Ten book.*

Sincerely,

Reginald Bosanquet

Reginald Bosanquet

*PS Perhaps you would like to write the Foreword

Bibliography

If you have enjoyed reading this book, here is a list of some further titles you may care to enjoy:

Non-Fiction
Mowing the Lawn by H.R.H. The Duke of Edinburgh
How to Spell by The Quoon
Tree Diseases and You (A thrilling account of life in Basingstoke)
Make Youself Hoarse
The Home Book of Ruptures (Illus.)
Teach Yourself Rubbish (Not available in Canada)
The Girl's Book of Toad-Sexing
Toad-Sexing for Toddlers
Toad-Sexing as a Money-Earner
It Pays to Increase Your Toad-Sexing
Toad-Sexing Can be Fun
Teach Yourself Toad-Sexing
My Life with a Toad-Sexer
Regular Toad-Sexing
Toad-Sexing for Married Couples
Toad-Sexing at Sixty
You and the Toad
The Spanish Toad-Sexer
Toad-Sexing all the Year Round
Indoor Toad-Sexing
A Midsummer Night's Toad-Sexing (Play)
Toad-Sexing in the Car
Lumps You Can Do Things With
Bursting – a First Primer
Magnetism Made Dull
Your Health and the Cat
Vegetables I Will Never Forget (with a foreword by U. Thant)
How to Get Drunk for 6p (De Luxe edition only: £8)
Fun with Parrots
Fun with the Duke of Edinburgh
Fun with a Loose Chair Cover
Fun with Practically Anything
Forever Toad-Sexing
Keep Breathing (No. 1 in our *How to Live* series)
Putting Your Leg in The Air Vol. 1
Putting Your Leg in The Air Vol. 2
How to Get Up
Forty Miles of Anger (The True Facts about the River Police)
Fun with the River Police (Sequel to *Forty Miles of Anger*)
Living in Hendon (One of our *Aid for The Handicapped* Books)
How To Have Lunch With Doris Lessing
Stop Yourself Toad-Sexing
The Boys' Book of Boils and Sores
Sex Hygiene Without Looking
Be a Sparrow (Includes free wings)
So You're Interested in Acne...
Things a Married Couple Should Know by Dr. & Mrs A. Kronberg & Jennifer Woods
Things a Married Couple Shouldn't Know by Dr. & Mrs A. Kronberg & John Woods
Pimples That Mean Success
You Can Taunt Cows

Fiction
Southern Region Timetable 1971

Historiography
Here is a list of some further histories you may care to enjoy:
Noonan's *History of Trees*
R. T. Sampson: *History of the Naughty People*
Winston Churchill's *A History of the English-Speaking Peoples*
Martin Bedford's *A Short History of Chairs, Tables and Pieces o Wood*
Kate Hepburn's *A History of the English-Speaking Publishers*
A Short History of History Books by R. T. Boredom
Carol Cleveland's *A History of Toad-Sexing*
R. Bosanquet: *A Shorter History of Newscasters*
A. Gardner: *A Longer History of Newscasters*
G. Honeycombe: *A History of L. Parkin*
M. Aspel: *The Longest History of Newscasters*
R. Dougall: *The Collected History of Newscasters*
R. Bosanquet: *A History of All Bloody Newscasters and For word Writers*

Biography
The Life and Times of Mrs Betty Rogers, 42, The Cottages, Ne Brighton, Cheshire by Mr Norman Robinson of 43, The Co tages, New Brighton, Cheshire
A Neighbour Remembers Mrs Rogers, by Mr Pules of 41, Th Cottages, New Brighton, Cheshire
The Charlie Cooke Book
The Appallingly Vile, Debauched and Drunken Life of a Friend Mine, oh all right, me (This should be under *AUTOBIO GRAPHY*. Ed.)
The Golden Days of Publishing (Tuesdays and Fridays) G. Strachan
Can I Have A Mention in Your Book? by Roger McGough
What About Us Then? by Mike McGear & John Gorman
A Life by A. Life
I Suppose You'll Do Another Reginald Bosanquet Joke by Bosanquet
No, Honest by Ed.

Autobiography
Here is a list of some further autobiographies you may care enjoy:
Mee, by Bertie Mee
The Sporting Life of a Ghost Writer, by Gary Sobers, Ton Docherty, George Best, Billy Wright, Brian Labone and Fra Lee
Stone Me, The Autobiography of St Stephen (all others are copies)
Here is the News by R. Bosanquet
My Life Already by Ikey Cohen

Hagiography
Here is a list of some further saints you may care to enjoy:
St Butch
St Francis of Near Assisi But Not the Bird Nut
St Paul the Whippet-Trainer
St Pancras
St Ation the Station
St Patron, the Patron Saint of Patrons
St Jules, the Patron Saint of St Jeremy
St None the Less
St Reginald, the Patron Saint of Foreword Writers